Dad #1, Dad #2

Dad #1, Dad #2

A Queerspawn View from the Closet

Natalie Perry

Red Cricket Press

Published by Red Cricket Press
5726 W. Centerbrook Drive
Boise, Idaho
83705
United States of America

Copyright © Natalie Perry 2017
First Edition 2017

All rights reserved
Except for brief excerpts for review purposes, no part of this book may be reproduced or used in any form without prior written permission from the publisher.

ISBN 978-0-9988756-0-6
eISBN 978-0-9988756-1-3
Library of Congress Control Number: 2017939748

Cover art and design: Jean Calomeni
Developmental editor: Cristen Iris
Copy and line editor: Jeri Walker
Proofreader: Liela Browne
Interior design and layout: Kiran Spees

www.redcricketpress.com

Dad #1, Dad #2: A Queerspawn View from the Closet is a work of nonfiction. Aside from family members, names and identifying details have been changed. Some dialogue has been recreated. The details of this book are true to the best of my present recollection.

To my family for teaching me how to love unconditionally and for understanding and supporting my desire to share our story.

I feel small sitting here
Look around
My heart aches for reasons
Unknown to me

Contents

Part 1: Boise, Idaho 1996-2002

Chapter 1: Coming Out 1
   The Dream 18

Chapter 2: Blending Families 23
   Memory 41

Chapter 3: Hiding in the Shadows 43
   Nothing Wrong 57

Chapter 4: Losing Faith 59
   Mother 71

Part 2: Leaving Idaho 2002-2011

Chapter 5: New York 81
   Ready 97

Chapter 6: Europe 103
   Forever Trapped 120

Chapter 7: Peace Corps 123
   Fallen 137

Chapter 8: AmeriCorps 139
Sin..152

Part 3: Returning Home 2011-2015
Chapter 9: Things Change 157
Lost..169

Chapter 10: Gay Marriage 171
People..182

Reflections 183
Notes..187
Bibliography 189

Part 1
Boise, Idaho 1996-2002

1 Coming Out

My mom has always said when my dad came out of the closet, we stepped in. I was only twelve, and it had already been a difficult year with several family illnesses and deaths. School had just ended, and we were enjoying the first days of summer in June of 1996 when I found myself sitting at the dining room table with my sister and parents for another family meeting.

My sister, Katie, and I knew something was going on between our parents, even though they never fought in front of us. Over the course of the year, many discussions had taken place behind closed doors. Sometimes they would get home after eating dinner out and sit in the car in the garage for over an hour. When they finally came in, their eyes were red and swollen from crying. Katie and I couldn't figure out what was happening, but we knew some major rifts had opened in their relationship. We also knew they would tell us when they were ready.

Overall, we thought our parents were happy. But as we sat at the dining room table that day, the sense of foreboding was great because we were finally going to learn the big secret.

"I am gay," my dad stated, starting the conversation.

Katie, who was three years older than me and understood what this meant, interrupted and asked, "You're getting a divorce then, right?"

My dad was taken aback as the speech he'd prepared was immediately moved from *gay* to *divorce*.

"Yes, we will be getting divorced," my dad replied. "But we will remain friends. We both love you and will always put you two first. You and Natalie are our priority."

I was totally confused. I had lived a fairly sheltered life growing up in Idaho and didn't really understand what it meant to be gay. When I asked, my dad told us this meant he liked men instead of women. In some ways, this confused me more because he'd married my mom. At the same time, I was worried about my dad. He was crying, not only because of telling us about the divorce, but because he was terrified we wouldn't love him anymore.

"I still love you Dad," I told him.

"Me too," Katie chimed in. "We can even help you prepare for dates!"

When it came to our parents dating, Katie and I wanted them to be happy and told each that if they met someone who brought joy to their life we would accept that person into the family. After these reassurances, there were more tears and hugs before the meeting ended and we left the table so my dad could get ready to move out.

We grew up with the concept of *table talk* meaning it was something we couldn't share outside the family. This is how our parents taught us what was appropriate to tell others and what was meant to stay in our home. They had made it clear this conversation wasn't safe to be shared. My dad was a judge for the Idaho State Court of Appeals. While he was originally chosen and sworn in by the governor, it was a position up for re-election every six years. Idaho is one of the most conservative states in the country; I've occasionally heard it described as the Deep South of the Northwest, which couldn't be more apt. We all knew if his sexuality became public he would lose his job, which created a lot of fear for our family. This affected how we lived our lives for many years. Despite the risk, my parents gave me permission to reach out to my sixth-grade teacher, who'd already seen me through a turbulent year.

I've been very fortunate to have some amazing teachers throughout my life, but Mrs. Smith was one of the most memorable and impactful teachers I ever had. The first day of school, she walked into class and wrote her home phone number on the board. Mrs. Smith told the class to write it down in our notebooks so we didn't lose it. She told us if we ever got ourselves in a situation during the school year and needed help that we were to call her, no matter what the time or day. She said if we ever needed someone to lean on and were too afraid to call our parents she would be there for us.

After I left the dining room table, I picked up the phone and called her. She was already familiar with the various family problems from the past year as she had been the rock I leaned on during my sixth-grade year. Shortly after school started my maternal grandmother became ill. She underwent surgery and ended up having a stroke on the operating table. It was touch and go for a while, but by Christmas she had started to heal.

Then in January, my paternal grandfather, Papa Ray, died two days after my birthday. My parents woke Katie and me up early in the morning, telling us they'd received a call he was sick. They were immediately flying to the hospital in Portland. I'll never forget how my stomach dropped. I knew without a doubt he was dead.

It was Martin Luther King Jr. Day, so we didn't have school. Since my parents left that morning, Katie and I were home by ourselves. It was an excruciatingly long day. The power had gone out, and we were having a hard time distracting ourselves without a TV to watch or music to listen to. We couldn't escape our worries and ended up questioning whether our grandpa was really okay. Katie was convinced Mom and Dad would call if something was seriously wrong. She didn't think they would wait until they returned home at the end of the day, but I wasn't so sure. I still couldn't shake the feeling from that morning.

I was close to my grandpa. He'd always wanted a grandson but wound up with three granddaughters (my only male cousin wasn't born until shortly before his death). I grew up as a complete tomboy, which was great for my grandpa but frustrating for my mom. She used to buy me a new outfit every Easter and would be so excited to dress me up. She then insisted on taking a picture before I was allowed to go outside because she knew I'd be covered in dirt within minutes.

I always loved spending time with Papa Ray. Whenever I visited he would take me back to his shop where we would trace patterns on wooden planks and then use the electric saw to carve flowers. He was the handiest person in my family and would often do small repair projects when he visited us in Idaho. He taught me a lot over the years that helped me to be self-sufficient and take care of small things around the house. He also understood my love for learning about people and cultures different from my own. He supported my obsession with Native Americans and used to buy me books on the history of indigenous groups in Idaho as well as those across the country.

Only my mom returned at the end of the day; my dad had chosen to stay in Portland with my Grandma Izzy. When my mom walked through the door by herself my suspicions were confirmed. They hadn't wanted to deliver the bad news over the phone, but Papa Ray had passed earlier in the morning. They didn't even make it to the hospital in time to say goodbye.

I felt guilty about my grandfather's death. I'd been the last person in my immediate family to talk to him because he had called for my birthday. At the end of our conversations I would always say, "I love you" and would wait for his normal response, "I love you more." It had been that way for as long as I could remember, but on that day he didn't say it. He sounded tired and I wondered if something could be wrong, but I didn't ask him about it and I didn't say anything to my parents. Two days later when he died I wondered if things would be different if I had said something that night.

Three months later, I was practicing piano in the hallway when the phone rang. My mom answered and listened for a moment before bursting into tears in the kitchen. My uncle Chris had committed suicide after murdering his ex-girlfriend. He was an alcoholic and suffered from depression. Twice over the previous months he had called my mom, threatening to kill himself. My mom tried for hours to calmly talk to him, but in his drunken state he was angry with the world and convinced the whole family hated him and that he had nothing to live for. When he would eventually hang up, she'd frantically called her other siblings who lived in the area to find someone to check on him. Some in the family tried to get him help but he was resistant. I think other family members thought he would never actually do anything to hurt himself. Ultimately, he could never get over his most recent breakup. In April of that year, he took a gun to the glass factory where his ex-girlfriend worked, forced her into the bathroom, and shot her, orphaning her two sons, before turning the gun on himself.

Being twelve and dealing with the deaths of two family members in a three-month period, especially when one was a murder-suicide, was particularly difficult to process. I would often stay late after school talking with Mrs. Smith. I felt comfortable with her and would share everything going on in my life. She was an incredible listener and would always let me talk and cry and work through my feelings. In some ways, I felt more comfortable with her than with my parents because I knew they were hiding something from me at the time. I still think of Mrs. Smith as my guardian angel who looked after me during that year of tumultuous change. On the last day of school, she took me aside and told me that even though she was no longer my teacher, she was still there for me if I ever needed to talk about anything that had happened over the past year or about things to come. Little did she know that it would only be a matter of days before she would hear from me again.

The night after that family meeting, I called and I told her I needed to talk. I'm sure she could tell from the quiver in my voice that something else had happened. She didn't ask me any questions and just told me she could meet me in her classroom the next day. Summer vacation had just started, and I'm sure she was looking forward to her own plans, but there she was going above and beyond and still allowing me to look to her for support.

I barely made it through the classroom door before I burst into tears, and she wrapped me in an enormous hug. Through the tears and over the next couple of hours, I managed to tell her about my parents' impending divorce and my dad being gay. Even though it was a private topic, and I understood I had to be careful about who I told, I had no hesitation in being honest with her—especially since my parents had said it was okay for me to tell her. She already knew all the horrible things my family had experienced over the past year and had never betrayed my confidence. I had no doubt she would protect my secret without judgment.

When I finally left, she reminded me that I could continue to call her whenever I needed. Despite the offer, I didn't call her again. I've run into Mrs. Smith a few times over the years, and she's always asked how I'm doing. Even after all these years she remembered me (although after being a teacher myself I believe I was the kind of student who was rather difficult to forget) and seemed to still genuinely care about my well-being. She even asked about my family and whether my parents ever remarried. Once my dad met his partner, Jerry, she inquired about him as well.

To this day, I'm grateful for her love and support over that year. I think her example helped me become a better teacher myself when

I later went into education. I believe I had more empathy and compassion toward my students and understood when they were going through challenging times because I had a teacher who had shown me such support.

※

The summer of the divorce was difficult. There were many things I didn't understand about my dad's sexuality and how my parents' divorce would affect our family. I had never met anyone who was gay and while my dad said he'd determined that he liked men, I wasn't entirely sure I knew what that meant. I had several friends whose parents were divorced and none of them had amicable relationships. The kids I knew felt torn and were often used as pawns during the divorce.

I spent a lot of that summer staying at my friend Mary's house. She and I had been friends since my family had moved to Boise three years prior. Her dad died when she was younger, so her mom raised Mary and her younger brother as a single parent. They were a close family, although much less strict than my own.

When I first told Mary my parents were getting divorced, she was shocked. "But they get along so well! They never even fight." I learned to get used to this response as everyone saw my parents as the perfect couple. I struggled with what to tell people. I couldn't announce to the world my dad was gay, so I would say, "Yeah, well, they've just grown apart." It seemed such a simple explanation for such a complicated situation, but usually people accepted it and didn't ask many follow-up questions.

Mary's mom, Sarah, welcomed me into their home and told me I could spend as much time there as I wanted. I took her up on the offer. I spent my days hanging out with Mary and had several sleepovers where I spent the night on the couch.

I wanted to tell Mary and her mom the truth; she was the closest friend I had at the time. I seriously contemplated it a few times but knew we needed to be careful about who we told. I didn't know how a young girl my age could make my dad lose his job, but I understood that that's what everyone was afraid of. Every time I thought about sharing my secret with Mary, I remembered a previous conversation. We were sitting in her room listening to music when "Come to My Window" by Melissa Etheridge came on the radio.

"Ugh! I hate her music," Mary said.

"Really? I love this song. I think she has a cool voice."

"Yea, but you know she likes girls, right? When I know she's singing about that it grosses me out. I can't stand listening to her music knowing that."

At the time, I didn't know my dad was gay. I also didn't really care who Melissa Etheridge was singing about. I liked the song and for me, it was that simple. I didn't need to delve into the details of a musician's love life to know the details of the lyrics. I just knew it was something I liked singing along to.

The conversation stuck with me, though, probably because it was one of the first times I can recall someone speaking negatively about homosexuality. When I found out about my dad and our family talked about being careful about who we told, I knew I couldn't share with Mary. I knew it would disgust her, and I didn't want to lose her as a friend.

Years later, when I was in high school, Mary heard about my dad from the first person I finally shared the secret with and she told her mom. I will never forget the day they asked me about it. We were in the car and Mary mentioned the divorce and my dads. We were almost to her house, but Sarah pulled the car over to the side of the road, put it in park, and turned to me in the backseat with tears streaming down her cheeks.

"I'm so sorry, Natalie. So terribly sorry that you felt like you couldn't tell us about your family. I can't imagine what it must have been like for you all these years, holding that inside, not knowing who to trust. I'm so sorry because I wish you'd known that you could be honest with us. We care for you, and you will always be welcome in our home. I don't want to push you to share anything that you're not comfortable with, but please, always know that you can tell us anything. Please don't feel like you have to hide anything from us ever, okay?"

By the time she finished her speech, Mary and I were both crying as well. I could barely stammer, "Okay. And thank you. You have no idea how much that means to me."

It was, and still is, one of the greatest moments of acceptance I've experienced. They had no idea about of all the negative, careless reactions I'd received over the past four years. To have someone I desperately wanted to tell, but was too afraid to be honest with, tell me it was okay and didn't make a difference, was one of the greatest gifts they could've given me. I was sixteen, and it was the first time I was happily surprised by the response of someone I'd been so afraid to trust. It also made me think maybe I shouldn't be afraid to do so in the future.

My parents' divorce was difficult, but dealing with my dad's sexuality was more so. There were several things I didn't understand. How can you love someone and then realize later that you're gay? What makes someone gay and why are they that way? What does that even mean exactly? How do gay people have sex? If my dad's gay, then am I gay, too?

I am very fortunate to have the family I do. My mom is a social worker, and her attitude toward parenting can be summed up as—if you're old enough to ask, you're old enough to know. She had proven we could go to her with anything, and she would always have an honest conversation with us. One of my first memories of this is when I was six or seven. One of my friends told me sex was when a man put his penis between a woman's breasts. I didn't believe her so I went home and asked my mom. Because of her calm demeanor when I first went to her, I was always comfortable going to her in the future. In fact, as I got older many of my friends would look to me to provide answers about sex, protection, and drugs. Many were never comfortable going to their own parents, and they knew I had an open relationship with mine and would always receive correct information. (This was before looking things up online was a regular practice). Looking back, I realize many of my questions about the divorce and my dad's sexuality must have been uncomfortable and painful for my mom, but she never once balked and always answered them as honestly as she could.

After the Melissa Etheridge incident with Mary, but prior to my dad coming out to the family, I'd asked my mom if it was okay to be gay. At the time, she told me no, that it was a sin against God. After she and my dad started dealing with his sexuality, she came back to me to tell me that she'd been mistaken and that there was nothing wrong with being gay. She was worried if I thought being gay was a sin it would affect my relationship with my dad. Obviously, the conversation didn't make too great of an impression on me; while my mom would later talk of the anguish she felt about her original response, I don't even remember the discussion.

While my mom struggled with these conversations, so did my dad. He was raised in a Catholic family, so he was told being gay was a sin. When he and my mom were still dating, they took a short break from the relationship. He was hesitant about getting married. He talked to many of his friends who encouraged him to take that step; they all said my mom was perfect for my dad. He also spoke with his pastor who told him breakups were normal and natural in the dating process and that they should get married. In retrospect, my dad said part of his hesitation was probably due to his internal struggle, but he'd never acknowledged his sexuality or shared his struggles with anyone at that point. When he talked to my mom after sixteen years of marriage, she was the first person he'd ever confided in. Before that he had never trusted anyone enough to talk to them about his conflicted feelings.

My parents went to counseling for about a year before my dad came out to us. They each had individual sessions and sessions as a couple. My dad was trying to figure out his sexuality and what it meant to be a gay husband and father. They were both trying to figure out what this meant for them as a couple and for us as a family. I don't know the details of that year and honestly, I don't need to.

My dad had a lot of guilt over his sexuality and how it would affect us. But he also felt respect and obligation to the family unit and didn't want to break us up, so he was willing to stay married. It was actually my mom who asked for the divorce. She said neither one of them would be truly happy staying married and shouldn't settle for *happy enough*. She knew she couldn't spend the rest of her life waking up next to someone who might one day regret staying married. She knew she deserved better than that; she deserved to be with someone who loved her wholeheartedly.

My dad came out to his parents before Papa Ray died. He had been writing letters to his dad for months, generally talking about life, reality, acceptance, and change. When Papa Ray and Grandma Izzy decided to come to Boise for a visit, my dad knew his body showed his stress as he'd lost weight, leaving his already small form frail and gaunt. It was time to tell his parents, since they were worried about his health. My mom insisted on being there because she wanted to support him, and also be able to answer any questions his parents may have had. They met in his chambers at the Court of

Appeals over the weekend since the location would allow a private and comfortable place for the four of them to talk.

When he told them that he was gay, Izzy burst into tears, hugged him and asked, "Is that all? I thought you were going to tell us you were dying!"

Papa Ray didn't hesitate. He walked up to my dad and threw his arms around him. "You're still my son," he stated. He also told my dad that his letters had sounded just like the ones he'd gotten from his brother, Bill, when Bill had come out to him. Despite my Grandma Izzy's strict Catholic upbringing, she and Papa Ray were both completely accepting of my dad. They believed in love and compassion and always supporting their children. Since my grandpa passed soon after that, I knew it brought some peace to my dad to hear those words of acceptance.

Even though the conversation with his parents had gone well, my dad was still scared to tell Katie and me. He was terrified we wouldn't love him anymore. Sitting at the table that day when he made the announcement is the only time I've ever seen him truly afraid. And for him to be that fearful of his own daughters and our reactions was heart-wrenching. I can't imagine being petrified of being honest with your own family for fear of their disapproval.

My parents had always raised us to love and respect everyone. They were fond of saying, "The world would be a very boring place if everyone was the same." While there may be people in the world we don't understand, it isn't our place to judge. We should always treat everyone with respect and compassion, even when it is challenging. Even though we had this education, this was one of the first times in my life when I was put in a position of choosing whether I would follow these lessons. While Katie and I loved our dad and consoled him by telling him that this didn't change anything, that he would always be our dad, and we would always love him, we soon learned that not everyone in our lives would feel the same way.

My dad was raised Catholic, but my mom didn't grow up in a religious household. My maternal grandfather was an alcoholic, and her mother had difficulty raising nine children, basically on her own. As a result, my maternal grandmother spent much of my mom's childhood being emotionally, mentally, and physically abusive to her kids. My mom escaped her childhood through books and became the first person in her family to go to college. Since she had no family support, she enrolled herself and paid for it with scholarships and money earned by working.

My parents found the Presbyterian Church where they were married while still dating. They were part of a young adults group and very active. They both fell in love with the church and decided to become part of the congregation. They remained members after marrying and raised Katie and me in it while we were still living in Lewiston, Idaho. When our family later moved to Boise, they continued to follow the Presbyterian faith and found a church they liked in town.

Back in the 1990s the Presbyterian Church was divided on homosexuality, so they left it up to each congregation to decide if homosexuals would be allowed to worship there. There were two Presbyterian churches in Boise at the time, one that accepted the LGBTQ community and one that didn't. We soon found out we belonged to the church that didn't.

Since my parents were both people of faith, in addition to seeking counseling the year before their divorce, they sought guidance from the church. My dad was an Ordained Elder, which meant he was able to serve communion, counsel others, and serve on boards. Once it was determined my dad was gay and my parents were divorcing, the church told him that he could no longer exercise the rights of his position. My dad, and by extension we were not welcome to fully participate as we always had before.

I've spent the last twenty years telling people I was kicked out of my church. It wasn't until writing this book that I had a conversation with my dad and understood the specifics of what happened. I brought this up with my sister too, who told me that she'd never felt as if we'd been ousted. She also pointed out that whether we were actually asked to leave or simply made to feel so unwelcome that we left on our own, the end result was the same.

Hearing the difference in perception regarding this situation twenty years later made me realize my feelings about the situation were probably largely influenced by the fact I didn't understand these nuances. At the time, I was twelve. I knew we had been accepted and happy in the church and now that my dad was gay we weren't welcome. That was all I really understood, so for me I've always felt as if we were kicked out.

Thinking back on this experience and the different ways people in my family view it now highlights an important point. The age of children during these pivotal life events affects how much they understand and how they perceive a situation. If a child is too young to understand the details, they will explain it in a simplified way that makes sense to them. After twenty years, it's hard for me to describe this situation in another way. I'm glad I now understand the particulars of what happened, but it doesn't erase the perception I've held for so many years.

While my dad's Catholic family was completely accepting of his sexuality, not everyone in my mom's family was. Several in her family had *found God* much later in life and adopted quite conservative views. One such person was her dad. As a strong conservative, born-again, fundamentalist Christian, he believed homosexuality was a sin and that my dad was going to hell. He also took it one step further and believed anyone who didn't agree with this mentality, anyone who thought homosexuality was okay, was also a sinner and going to hell. His views included my mom, as well as, my sister and me, because he couldn't support us being raised in a family where we were taught that homosexuality wasn't a sin. So, at twelve years old my grandfather disowned me because my dad was gay and I still loved him.

One of the most amazing things about my parents' divorce was how adamantly they wanted to put Katie and me first and do what was best for us, regardless of how difficult this made things for the two of them. My mom got the equity in the house and every investment account, which they cashed in so she would have sufficient money to start over. She bought a small home in the same neighborhood so we wouldn't have to switch schools. During this time, my dad lived in a one-bedroom apartment until he could afford to buy his own home. Katie and I kept up with our normal extracurricular activities too. I kept my art lessons and Katie kept her voice lessons. My parents wanted as few things to change as possible.

Since my dad was a judge and my parents were splitting amicably, they decided to have a lawyer-free divorce. My parents had outlined divorce paperwork early on in case that date came. They kept it on a shelf in their closet, continually updating it throughout their time in counseling, so if they decided to get a divorce it would be easy, amicable, and fast. My parents agreed to all the terms including shared custody. There were no rules about how many days per week we would stay with each parent or how we would split the holidays. We were to move freely between the two homes and kept clothes, etc. at each house so we didn't have to pack our stuff back and forth.

The only firm ground rule was that we weren't allowed to leave one house in anger to go to the other. As a teenager, there were times this rule was extremely frustrating. But looking back, I've always been grateful that my parents had the foresight to not give Katie and me any opportunity to pit them against each other. Because they agreed to everything, it didn't take my dad long to draft the paperwork. The divorce was finalized just over two months after he had moved out.

After everything that had occurred over the past year, my parents were concerned about how Katie and I were handling it. They decided to put us both in counseling. Even though most people think we're twins, my sister and I actually couldn't be more different. We'd be an interesting case study for the nature versus nurture debate. While my sister's very introverted and decided to continue counseling for a few months, I only attended once. I'm not opposed to counseling; I believe it can be beneficial to have people to talk to about the struggles in our lives. But my extroverted, heart on my sleeve personality had thrown itself into my writing and preferred that coping mechanism, so I told my parents I didn't want to go anymore.

To my parents' credit, they didn't force me. My mom would tell me later she never worried about me emotionally because I always shared how I was feeling. I'm a bit of an open book. I turned to writing poetry instead. While I've never been a fan of journaling, I found poetry to be an outlet for everything I was dealing with. It quickly became not only my voice, but my therapy. I found myself writing to heal.

Despite only attending one session, counseling did bring up one question that I mentioned earlier. When you have gay parents, I think most people will question their own sexuality at an earlier age. I needed to figure out, if my dad was gay, then was I too?

Generally, straight people don't think about their sexual orientation. There is no big struggle for them to realize or come out as straight. If my dad wasn't gay, I probably never would have questioned this myself. I was only twelve, but I'd already started to think certain boys were cute and liked it when they paid special attention to me.

Yet when I found out about my dad's sexuality, I started to wonder about my own. Did I really like boys? Or did I just think I liked them, because I was supposed to? My dad had been confused enough about his sexuality to marry a woman only to later realize he was gay. Could I be in the same situation? I spent months looking at different boys and girls at school wondering if I could be attracted to them or if I wanted to kiss them. This bi-curiousness was a phase. I'd never had a boyfriend before, but there was one boy at school who gave me a funny feeling in my stomach when I was around him. I realized I had a bit of crush and ultimately, I found I really did like boys.

This questioning of sexuality, even as a straight person, is something I think children with gay parents can experience because we've been exposed to more types of family structures. We realize more options exist in the world and truly want to find where we fit. I also think this idea of finding our *fit* is even more prominent when one comes from a family that is continually told that as a unit they don't fit into society. For those of us who are told our families are wrong, we can question more strongly what we believe is right.

After the divorce, my mom still had to work through the reality that her sixteen-year marriage had ended. While it was challenging for my dad to accept his sexuality and his new life as a gay man, my mom had to learn to fall out of love with the person she always thought she'd spend the rest of her life with. This became even more of a struggle when, a mere month after their divorce, my dad met Jerry, the man who would later become his husband.

The Dream

I wished and prayed
That sober he'd stay
But dreams don't come true
When no one wants it but you

I wrote him letters
I called on the phone
But inside his head
No one was home

So my family tried too
They did all they could
Yet he still was drinking
Not listen he would

Finally one day
When we couldn't help him
He went and he entered
That place so dim

He was so drunk
His heart had failed
We couldn't reach him
Not even with bail

For he went beyond that
He went to his death
I was there standing
Where there was nothing left

He had taken a life
So precious, so pure
For this terrible disease
There is no cure

Yet, still even worse
There was more to come
And when I heard it
My heart went numb

The life he had taken
Was not just his
He had taken another
One that had kids

She was innocent
Naive and sweet
She sadly died wishing
They did not meet

He went to work
She was shot in the head
By the end of the night
They were both dead

Believe it or not
It's still not done
With what happened next
The peace was gone

The law suits came
Suing for all we were worth
Her family was upset
He'd taken their prize from birth

But what could we do
Certainly not bring her back
What were they to get
From their law pack

And after all
These events had finished
There was sorrow still
It would not diminish

These feelings I was fighting
I could only ask "Why?"
I couldn't stand it any longer
I broke down to cry

The healing process is hard
Delicate with danger
For you have to realize
It happened from anger

Chris was angry
He decided to drink
Now he is gone
And our souls sink

So for my poor uncle
Sad it may seem
But the hardest part is
I don't wake up from this dream

2 Blending Families

My dad and Jerry had met before at the gym but hadn't seen each other in over a year until they ran into each at the Flying M, a local coffee shop my dad frequented. On that August day, my dad introduced himself again and found out Jerry had recently split from his partner. My dad gave Jerry his business card and asked him to call if he'd like to have coffee together sometime. Although they'd seen each other around, Jerry had no idea my dad was a judge until reading his card. Jerry agreed to call, although he didn't realize my dad was gay. It wasn't until a few weeks later when he called my dad that Jerry realized something was different.

A couple weeks later Jerry called my dad and scheduled a coffee date for the tenth of September. They caught each other up on where they were in life. As those familiar with the LGBTQ community know, gay relationships can move quickly, so it wasn't long before Jerry came over.

My dad invited Jerry to the apartment for dinner, a movie, and to meet us girls. He brought his cat, Crissy. Katie and I were excited to meet Jerry; when he pulled in we were waiting for him and the cat on the curb. Crissy was leash trained. "Can I walk her to the apartment?" I asked. Jerry smiled and handed me the leash.

We spent a nice evening together having dinner and getting to know each other. At the end of the night, Jerry was unsure how to say goodbye to Katie and me. He didn't know if he should shake our hands or hug. I could sense that he was struggling so I told him, "We're Perrys. We don't shake hands; we hug." He broke out in a huge smile and gave us each a hug goodbye.

A few weeks later we all attended a local Renaissance fair. As we were leaving, Jerry was walking with Katie ahead of my dad and me. I asked my dad, "If we were going to have two dads, should we call you Dad Number One and Dad Number Two?" Jerry overheard the question and it warmed his heart.

Jerry had known he was gay since high school, so he grew up with the idea he wouldn't necessarily have kids. In some ways, he was pleasantly surprised my dad had two daughters. He would now have the opportunity to be a parent, but was also more than a little unsure of what having two teenage daughters would be like.

෴

Jerry's last long-term relationship had lasted for seven years and ended when he realized his partner wasn't on the same page and never would be. He'd always wanted to be married and to have a home and children. Jerry knew at the time that a gay marriage wouldn't be legal, but to him being in a real relationship was more about two people being committed to each other day in and day out. After years of discussions and ups and downs Jerry had ended the relationship. At that time, he swore off men and decided to focus on finding himself.

My dad and Jerry had been together for a couple months when things got serious. They were downtown one night when my dad told Jerry that he loved him. "You don't have to say it if you're not ready yet." Jerry knew he loved my dad but was freaked out because of his past relationships. They stayed up late that night discussing life plans, and Jerry explained what marriage looked like to him. He ended up giving my dad a list of conditions: commitment, a ring, ceremony (even if it wasn't legally binding), and a house that they bought together. He wanted a life together.

After Jerry finished his list, he asked my dad if he had any conditions. My dad said he didn't; he agreed with everything Jerry had said. He realized how deeply Jerry had been hurt in the past and told him if he gave him the chance, my dad would love him and never intentionally hurt him. My dad told Jerry he would do it all. "I'm ready, so you just let me know when you're ready."

It took Jerry four days to call my dad. A few days before Christmas, my dad's phone rang at the office and Jerry asked him what he was doing. "Just working," my dad replied. "How about you?"

"I was wondering if you would meet me at the jewelry store," Jerry said.

"Yes, I'll head that way in a few," my dad said.

"I'll be the guy in the red coat with the big smile on his face."

My dad responded, "I'll be the guy in the brown coat with an even bigger smile."

෴

We didn't spend our first Christmas together as a family of five. It had only been a few months since the divorce. While things were going well with my dad and Jerry, my mom was still trying to move on after the divorce. I didn't really understand why my mom was still so sad. I've always been fairly adaptable. Once my parents got divorced I started to adjust to the new situation. I didn't understand why it was taking my mom a little longer.

That first Christmas, my mom didn't even decorate our new house. She did eventually put up a tree, which she only did for Katie and me. She said we were the only reason she was able to work through the pain. This was the only holiday from all my childhood memories when it didn't seem like a time to celebrate.

After the holidays, and after being together for four months, my dad and Jerry flew to San Francisco in January of 1997 for their commitment ceremony. It was a small service with just a few friends from Boise and San Francisco in attendance. While the ceremony was important to Jerry, he didn't care much about where or how they had their commitment, he just wanted his partner to promise him one hundred percent.

At the time, the United States had just started the epic battle for gay marriage that's lasted for the past twenty years. It was originally sparked by the Hawaiian Supreme Court in 1993 when it ruled that denying same-sex couples the right to marriage violated the Equal Protection Clause of their Constitution.[1] During the following years, there was a severe backlash out of fear this would lead to legalizing gay marriage across the country. In 1996, President Clinton denied the federal benefits of marriage to same-sex couples by passing the Defense of Marriage Act (DOMA).[2] A couple years later, the voters of Hawaii approved an amendment to their state constitution banning same-sex marriage. In the years to follow several other states followed suit.

Based on the existing controversy over gay marriage in the country, my dads elected to have their commitment ceremony without inviting the immediate family, which they later both regretted. Our family managed to be a little mischievous and get them back for their choice. Jerry's mom, Grandma Sharon, came over with her friend before Dad and Jerry got back to town and helped us booby trap their apartment. We put cellophane over the toilet and faucet of the kitchen sink and short-sheeted their bed.

They returned to Idaho a committed couple, although not officially married, and Katie and I had two dads. I was happy for them but also a little disappointed they refused to do anything to change their last names. Katie and I used to joke with them, and I would plead with Jerry to change his. I really wanted him to be Jerry Perry.

When my dad first asked my mom to meet Jerry, she declined. Because my mom was still in pain and learning to move on after the divorce she didn't want to meet Jerry right away. While she did want to meet him and support their relationship, she was also self-aware enough to know she wasn't ready for this step. It was important to wait until she could give Jerry a fair chance. She was afraid if she met him too soon, she would judge him because she wasn't completely over my dad and the divorce.

She waited until after their commitment ceremony. It's funny to realize that after twenty years as a family together, no one remembers the day my mom and Jerry first met, although everyone seems to agree it was at a school function. What everyone does remember is that they became fast friends. Between school, piano and voice recitals, plus choir, the three of them were always at one of our performances. Within months, they'd figured out a system where my mom would go to the event to save seats while my dad and Jerry would go to Starbucks to get three coffees. They would sit together at every event from that day forward.

My mom felt relieved after meeting Jerry. She recognized he was just like her in personality and demeanor. Both are patient and have a calming effect on others, not to mention great senses of humor that provide endless entertainment for our family. My mom told us later that in some ways this validated my parents' relationship and made it easier for her to gain closure on their life as a married couple. Their divorce had nothing to do with her personally, but rather that she was a woman and my dad truly was gay. She took it as a compliment to her and their relationship that he found someone else just like her to be in his life.

Over the years my mom and Jerry have become close friends on their own. The two of them used to occasionally meet during the lunch hour to go shopping or for coffee to spend a few hours chatting. They found similarities in their small idiosyncrasies such as being big on birthdays, loving celebrations, and having strong commitments to giving to others. My mom also had an obsession with feeding others and Jerry loved to eat. Her monster cookie recipe was popular with friends and family, so she made it a couple times during the year. She initiated a tradition of texting Jerry at 10:00 at night when she got done baking, knowing he'd drive over to pick up cookies even though my dad was already in bed.

Now that my dad and Jerry were "married," they had to find a place to live. Buying their first house together became an exciting adventure. Jerry, the long-time bachelor, who only had a bottle of ketchup in his fridge for the entire four months of their courtship, and my dad, made it their goal to find a place within the same school district as our mom's house and one that would have enough space for the entire family.

My dad and Jerry finally bought their first home together in March 1997. It was an entertaining experience for both of them as they learned more about each other's wants and quirks. When it came time to look at houses, my dads hired a gay real estate agent as they were more comfortable with someone who understood their situation. My dad looked at the options first and then only took Jerry to those that made the shortlist. Dad has always tried to explain to real estate agents that Jerry can be quite particular. But it was still a rude awakening the first time the agent pulled up to a place and Jerry refused to get out of the car.

"Darrel, why would you bring me here?"

Before my dad could respond, the real estate agent interjected, "It's very nice inside. Let's go in and take a look around."

"Darrel, I'm not living in this shithole."

At this point the agent looked at my dad, "Okay, I think I'm beginning to understand his taste now."

They finally found a home that matched both of their preferences and had enough space for the family. We moved in on the first of

March, and this became our own family holiday: Perry-Marmon Day. We still celebrate this annually, marking the day we officially became a family.

Moving in with Jerry, who's a bit of a clean freak and perfectionist, was highly entertaining. On move-in day, I walked past the main bathroom to see him with his face three inches from the wall, paintbrush in hand.

"What are you doing?" I asked.

"Touching up the paint," he answered.

"Um ... okay. I think the wall looks fine."

"You don't see these spots on the wall? Right here?" he asked pointing.

I leaned in closely but couldn't see anything, which I told him.

"Really? Right here," he said pointing again.

I looked again. "Nope, I still don't see anything, but have fun with that." I left him to it, muttering the word *crazy* under my breath as I walked away.

Anytime families are blending, there's a need for compromise. The deeper families are into their own customs and culture, the more compromise is needed. Jerry never knew if he'd have kids, and while he was great with his nieces and nephews, he was usually better with them in small doses. He was used to having nice furniture and fragile décor, and he fully expected when he told a child to sit in one place for them to stay there. At this point, Katie and I were both teenagers so it was going to take a little extra finessing for this transition to go smoothly. One example is that Jerry wanted to come home to peace and quiet while he adjusted from his busy day at work. But Katie and I were always ready to talk about our days the minute he came through the door. At the time, we didn't understand why he needed time to unwind, although he kept telling us that one day we would. Now that we're adults, we do.

For years, Jerry had been a nurse working on the inpatient oncology floor at a local hospital. He had always loved his work and the flexible hours, but he also didn't anticipate he would ever have a family.

Jerry had realized he was gay in the fifth grade. He didn't fully understand what this initially meant, but he knew he didn't like girls the same way his other male friends did. He first experienced bullying in the sixth grade, which continued throughout junior high. This was the first time he heard the word *fag*. He looked it up and then began reading everything he could find to help him understand. He went to the local library and checked out books on homosexuality, lesbians, transsexuals, and more. Upon reading these books, he realized he had the same thoughts and feelings and determined he was homosexual.

Acknowledging he was gay threw him into a depression, and he began a mission to change himself. After years of unsuccessfully trying, he learned to accept himself for who he was. He never discussed this journey with anyone while going through it. He decided he could move away from his family and friends after high school graduation and never have contact with them again so he could be himself and live his life.

During junior high, his sister, Debbie, started dating Ryan. Debbie came home one night and asked if Jerry would go to a movie with them and Ryan's sister, Jan. Debbie explained she needed him to go because Jan was a lesbian. He decided to go as her "date," and he and Jan became friends. She introduced Jerry to gay bars where he soon met other guys. This opened his eyes to a world he'd never known existed—right in Boise, Idaho. Jerry met a nice boy he then started dating. This prompted him to finally talk to his parents.

Jerry started with his mom. He explained he really needed to talk with her. She agreed to late one night after everyone else had gone to bed. After they sat on the sofa, Jerry couldn't get the words out and simply sat and cried for a long while. Sharon consoled him, and told him it couldn't possibly be that bad. Despite the assurance, Jerry was still fearful his family would disown him.

After not being able to speak for some time, Grandma Sharon said, "I'll ask some questions and you tell me if I got it, okay?"

"Okay," he managed to say.

"Did you get a girl pregnant?"

"No," he said. Inside he was thinking that would be easy compared to what he was about to share.

"Are you having problems with drugs, alcohol, kids at school?" The list went on for a while, and he kept saying no.

Finally, she stuttered, "Are you a ho- ho- homosexual?"

"Yes," Jerry replied. He was then able to open up and tell her everything. Grandma Sharon told him that she worried about him. Jerry has always had a tender heart, and she'd been concerned about how others would treat him. She advised him not to say anything to his friends and told him she was a little sad because she'd always thought he would make a great dad. Being gay meant he wouldn't have kids. She brightened as she added, "Your dad and I can help you adopt children." He was fortunate to have an incredibly accepting and supportive family.

Because he'd known he was gay from and early age, he knew he would never end up in a heterosexual marriage with kids. He also knew he probably wouldn't ever be allowed to adopt in his lifetime. And before my dad, he had never dated anyone with kids.

Jerry was working on a career change when he met my dad. While he loved nursing, his dream job had always been to be a flight attendant. He had been accepted into a program to become one shortly after their ceremony in San Francisco. However, by that point, his priorities had changed. He decided he no longer wanted a job that would mean working such odd hours, including evenings and weekends. If he was going to have a family, he wanted to be present in our lives. He ended up turning down the flight attendant program and left nursing. Instead he took a nine-to-five management position at the hospital. I don't know if I've ever told him, but that was the first time I realized he was going to be a real parent because he was already willing to make sacrifices for us kids.

※

A few months after my dads' commitment ceremony, we took our first family trip. It was June of 1997. My dad decided to take our whole family to an annual judges' conference in Sun Valley, Idaho and rented a two-bedroom condo. He thought it would be a good bonding experience.

We had a fantastic time. Around the conference events, we went horseback riding and ice skating. But when we returned home he and Jerry realized that it was a really big deal that they'd taken the trip together. My dad started getting calls from magistrate judges he knew from all around the state telling him to never do it again. My dad was told that by living in such a conservative and religious state, he was already in the spotlight because of his divorce and many people were already gossiping about him and the reasons for my parents' split.

At the time, my dad was hurt but has said he realized later those judges weren't being mean. They were trying to protect him. They reinforced the idea that if too many people found out he was gay someone would run against him when was up for reelection in 2000, and he would lose his job. They told him that he had to be more closeted and cautious about who saw him with Jerry and to never take Jerry to any other events or conferences around the state.

These conversations with his friends and colleagues helped set the tone for how he would handle election years in 2000 and 2006, and the anxiety he would feel as he waited to see if anyone would run against him. It also helped shape the way he and Jerry lived their lives from that point on.

Jerry never attended another event in the legal setting in Idaho. As a judge on the Court of Appeals, my dad was required to serve *term of court* where judges traveled around the state to hear cases. Since they were gone for a week, judges sometimes took their spouses, but this wasn't an option for my dad. He also never took Jerry to the annual Christmas parties. He sometimes attended by himself, which caused him to be lonely at events since almost everyone else attended as a couple. At times, he would drop off his contribution to the party in the afternoon so he could skip the event. And when it came time to attend the Governor's Ball every four years, my dad alternated taking Katie and me as his date.

We were all vigilant in our personal lives too. Katie compared living in Idaho to the Don't Ask, Don't Tell (DADT) military policy.[3] We acknowledged a degree of appropriate risk in our daily lives because we lived together as a family and would go out in public for school functions and family events. We couldn't hide completely, not if we chose to live a normal family life. But we all understood we wouldn't take any unnecessary risks.

Jerry acquired the skill of disappearing in public whenever people approached my dad. Fortunately, it was pretty obvious when people were work acquaintances as they always called him Judge Perry instead of using his first name. Whenever I told stories about Jerry, I always told people he was my uncle. In my lie, he lived in town but had never married. My mom and dad didn't have any other family in Boise so it made sense that he would spend his holidays with us.

That December we had our first real Christmas as a family. Decorating our tree was a learning experience for all of us. When I was younger I'd made my dad a bear ornament with my picture in the middle. We made them at school; it was around eight inches tall and five inches wide. My parents had bought Katie and me an ornament every year, so we always hung those on the tree along with the ones we'd made over the years. I proudly took out the large bear and put it right on the front of the tree. I'll never forget the look of confusion, horror, and disbelief on Jerry's face. He gently asked me, "Natalie, are you sure you want to put it there?"

Jerry was used to things being pretty. To him, a Christmas tree was supposed to be beautiful, elegant, and at least slightly fragile. My paper bear didn't quite fit the bill. He looked at my dad, quietly begging with his eyes to please fix it. When my dad took the ornament off to move it, I asked him what he was doing. "I'm moving it to a place of honor on the back of the tree. He can watch over the outlet and make sure the tree doesn't come unplugged."

At the time, his response bothered me a bit. I was the youngest child and used to getting my way. It was an adjustment to think my dad had a new person in his life just as important to him as we were. Even though I always liked to think I had him wrapped around my finger, I realized there would now be times when in a disagreement, he would side with Jerry. This was the first time I remember being aware I would sometimes have to compromise too.

This was the year we became a family of five. My dads, mom, Katie, and I started spending all holidays together because my parents didn't want to jostle us between homes. For birthdays, the guest of honor would pick the restaurant where we'd all meet. After dinner, we'd go back to my mom's because she would always make a homemade dessert of our choice to celebrate. For presents my parents set up a gift account that my dad would put a designated amount of money in each month, and my mom would withdraw and combine with her own money to buy gifts for the occasion. Every card and gift came from the three of them so there would be no competition for our love. They would always discuss gifts before my mom went shopping so they were all in agreement on what she would be buying. They also started signing all our cards, "Mom, Dad #1 and Dad #2."

My parents would also alternate hosting Thanksgiving and Christmas each year. When we were younger, it had been very important to my mom that we create our own family traditions. For my family, Christmas Eve is just as important as Christmas day, if not more so, because we spend the entire day together. We always go to a movie, which usually takes planning weeks in advance to find one we all agree on. After the movie, we go to a pizza joint for dinner because no one wants to cook before the big meal the next day.

After dinner, we go back to my mom's house where we read Christmas stories. Katie alternates between "Olive, the Other Reindeer" and "Angelina's Christmas." I have a book of Christmas traditions from around the world, and I share a new one each year. My dad always reads "The Night Before Christmas," and my mom finishes up with the story of Jesus from the Bible. After our stories, Katie and I each get to open one present. Our gift is always pajamas that my mom has already washed with Downy and sealed in a plastic bag to keep the smell. It's one of my favorite parts of Christmas because even now when I smell the pajamas every year it reminds me of childhood.

On our first Christmas with Jerry, we had to find a story for him to read as well. This was fun for Katie and me but a little nerve-racking for Jerry. He doesn't like to read in front of groups, not even small ones. He used to choose a story from one of the Christmas books when we were younger, probably because it was so important to us. But these days he usually opts out and instead just listens to the stories the rest of us share as he cuddles with my dad.

In 2002, my dad and Jerry decided they wanted to take us on a family trip for Christmas. As we all sat around the restaurant table for Easter brunch, we picked up our menus to find another homemade menu underneath. Opening it revealed an itinerary for Christmas in Mexico. This was one of my favorite Christmas stories, because people were often surprised they paid for the trip for all of us, including my mom. Many of my college friends, especially those with divorced parents, thought it was odd we would vacation together as a family of five. I mentioned this to my dad and Jerry at one point and they responded, "She's your mom, and we've always spent the holidays together. We would never take you kids away from your mom on Christmas, so of course she's included."

Our first Christmas was also important because it was when my dad started writing year-in-review letters to Jerry. The letter included all of their special moments from the year: family, friends, travel, and celebrations—whether they be funny, amazing, sad, or exciting. After all of us leave on Christmas Eve, Jerry stays up late and opens his letter. My dad goes to bed early, but says he always loves hearing Jerry gasp, cry, and laugh as he's reminded of all their big moments together. Jerry always says this is the best gift my dad gives him every year. Katie and I have never been allowed to read these letters, and they've become a joke over the years. Apparently, there are some embarrassing stories they don't want us reading until after they're dead. But we always talk about what a great book they will make someday.

Over the years, we've found several other things we had to compromise on when blending our families. Jerry didn't like sharing his clothes or food, and Katie and I would regularly raid our dad's closet and eat food off his plate. He also had a hard time the first time they high heels only to realize how difficult they were to walk in. He kept flipping his hair to keep it out of his face. As they left, Katie and I commented to each other on the certainty of some fun stories in the making by the end of the night.

The next day, when we got together to hear about their night, Jerry exclaimed, "It's so hard to be a woman! It took forever to go to the bathroom and I had so many runs in my pantyhose. How do women wear those with nails?" Katie and I just laughed.

Another lesson that Jerry learned over my teenage years was the importance of promises. I'm a big believer in celebrating life's accomplishments. When I was about fifteen I decided when I graduated high school I wanted to go skydiving. During this conversation, Jerry promised he would go with me, thinking I would never actually go through with it. As my senior year came to a close I told him it was time to look at dates so that we could plan our skydiving trip.

"Natalie, I don't really want to do that. I didn't think when we talked about this years ago, that you would actually want to do it," he said.

"But Jerry, you promised!" I told him.

Since he really didn't want to go, he followed up with my dad, telling him how scared he was and how it really wasn't something that he wanted to do. My dad gave him the same response, "Jerry, you promised. You never make promises to the girls unless you actually plan to follow through with them. You're committed."

A little begrudgingly, Jerry gave in and, at the end of the year, we made a reservation. As we got suited up, he kept telling me how terrified he was, "I don't know if I'm going to jump once we get up there," he kept telling me.

But once in the air, he did manage to hurtle himself out of the plane, although with a bit of screaming. When we both made it safely to the ground, I asked him what he thought. "Well, I'm happy

I can say I went through with it and can mark it off the bucket list, but I have absolutely no desire to ever do it again."

※

While there were many areas where we had to learn to compromise to blend our family, I also learned a lot from having Jerry in my life. He's very crafty and always nourished mine and Katie's artsy sides. He also taught me an important distinction about money. While my mom was extremely frugal and taught me how to budget and the value of a dollar, Jerry taught me the importance of investing in things that are important to me. I've never been someone who's spent much money on clothes, makeup, or accessories. But I've always loved bags, especially for travel.

When I was younger, I had a hard time spending what seemed like a lot of money at the time for quality luggage that would last a long time. I'll never forget Jerry telling me, "Will you use it and love it for years to come? Then it's worth the money, Natalie." I still sometimes have a hard time with this, but over the years I've invested in my college education, travel, volunteer work, a new car, and even this book. Every time is scary for me. But every time I ask myself that same question, "Is it worth the investment?" and this has helped me decide when it truly is.

In some ways, I think blending families was easier with gay dads. While straight families have so many rules regarding step families and what to call people because nobody wants to upset or offend others or have them feel like they're being replaced, we didn't have those same issues. The dynamics and jealousies can be different. Because Jerry was my dad's partner and he was the one to add Jerry to the family, my dad didn't feel threatened by us girls having another dad. At the same time, because he was another dad, my mom never felt like she was being replaced.

It's worth noting my family doesn't use the word *step* regarding anyone who's married into our family. Jerry isn't, nor has he ever been, my stepdad. His mom isn't my step grandma: neither are my aunts, uncles, or cousins. While there was never a discussion regarding how we categorize or title our family, we all just understood that for us, we are all simply family.

By the same token, my dad and Jerry also refused to use *ex* in talking about my mom. She was not an ex-wife. My dad and Jerry always referred to her as Katie and Natalie's mom or the girls' mom, and still do to this day.

This notion was strengthened when we met Jerry's family. I think they were all so happy he'd finally found someone who treated him well and that he wanted to spend his life with. His mom, siblings, nieces, and nephews all warmly welcomed us into their family and lives.

My dad's family was the same. A few months after moving to our new house, we took a trip to Portland to visit my dad's family. We were all supposed to get together at my aunt and uncle's home. When we arrived, everyone was there. They had ordered a wedding cake and wanted to have a reception with the entire family. They wanted us to know they loved and accepted us, and always would. They wanted Jerry to know he was welcome in our family and they accepted our gay household. For them, it changed nothing, we were family and always would be.

It was a distinct difference and relief from my maternal grandfather's reaction and the one I would encounter at school.

Memory

I remember
When you were lying in bed
Mother crying; father praying
I was wishing you were dead

I know you're flesh and blood
But the desire was still there
I couldn't keep it from coming
I couldn't force myself to care

It became apparent to me then
How much I hate you
How your life means nothing to me
How our relationship is through

How dare you disown me
When you never truly knew
What lies deep inside me
Has no connection to you

You base your beliefs on God
Tell me I should hate my father
Tell me that's what God wants
When you didn't even bother

To read the Book you idolize
And see what it really means
See what God really wants
But most of all, just see

That my father is a good man
While you choose to dwell
Disowning your own family
Will make you burn in hell

3 Hiding in the Shadows

Transitioning from one grade to another, especially elementary school to junior high school, can be challenging. Because I'm a social person, I was looking forward to branching out and meeting new people. I only had a handful of friends in elementary school; I still hadn't met many people I clicked with since moving to Boise back in 1993. When I started junior high I met a new group of people when I became acquainted with Brenda. She and I seemed to click immediately and became fast friends.

After a few months, I felt like I could trust her, and I decided to tell her about my family. One day after school I told her, "My dad's gay. That's why my parents divorced."

"Oh," was all she said. I was surprised she didn't have any questions. I went home thinking everything was okay.

The next morning, I got to school and Brenda pulled me aside. "You're no longer part of our group. Don't talk to us. We're not your friends anymore." With that she walked off leaving me standing in the hallway, stunned. That day, I ate lunch by myself, an outcast numb to everything going on around me. I realized what my family was so afraid of—anyone and everyone could reject us at any time without warning. Every new relationship I made could potentially end if I told people about my dads.

While I was angry and hurt by the situation at the time, I knew it wasn't really her fault. She was young, and I knew it wasn't her decision. She'd told her parents about my dads, and it was their words she was repeating. I knew there were many Mormons in Idaho, but I didn't know much about the religion. It took me awhile to figure out Brenda was Mormon and that her family believed homosexuality was a sin.

Since my dads' house was in the same neighborhood as Brenda's, our relationship was even more complicated. They lived less than a block away. It was fascinating how her mom would force a smile when she saw me outside in the front yard, yet wouldn't allow her daughter to be my friend.

After losing all my friends, I bounced around between different groups at school as I struggled to find people I fit in with. I had always been a social and outgoing child who enjoyed being around others. My mom used to love to tell her friends about taking me to the park when I was little. She said I used to march up to the kids in the sandbox and proclaim, "I'm Natalie, wanna play?" Losing my new friends was one of the hardest things I experienced in junior high.

I was also guarded after my experience with Brenda, which made it that much harder for me to trust people. Finally, in the eighth grade I met Cindy through a writing class. She was a year older than me and hung out with a group of outcasts, and in some ways, that felt normal to me. Since I'd been cast out of my group of friends, I thought maybe these were people who would accept me, which they did. I didn't share everything with them, but since Cindy was familiar with my writing she knew about some of my family experiences, such as my uncle's suicide and being disowned by my grandfather.

I was still afraid to be completely honest about my family with the whole group. It wasn't only that I had a hard time trusting others, but I'd also lost confidence in myself. I was no longer sure I could read people well enough to know whether they would judge me and my family.

While we had plenty of differences, my relationship with them solidified my view that those who live on the outskirts of society are more open to those who are different. Even though our differences weren't the same, we all knew what it meant not to be fully accepted by society.

Coping through my writing had its own challenges. I felt that the class was a safe place for me to express myself, so I wrote poetry about my life experiences. But when I wrote about suicide my teacher reported me to the school counselor. I was taken out of class and sent to the counselor's office.

She showed me the poem I'd written. "Natalie, I'm concerned about you and your writing. I received this poem from your teacher. Can you tell me about it?"

"It's a poem I wrote about my uncle and his suicide," I answered. "Is that a problem?"

She dodged my question. "Do you ever think about suicide, Natalie?"

I sat there shocked, unable to answer for a moment.

Since my uncle had committed suicide after murdering his ex-girlfriend, I'd come to relate the two in my mind. As I sat trying to focus on what she was saying, all I could think was whether she was thinking I could really be like him. That I was possibly unstable. That I could potentially hurt not only myself but other people as well.

While I understood the challenges teachers face, it was damaging to me at the time. Writing was my therapy, and I had several questions and issues I was trying to work though. Poetry was the one outlet where I felt I had a voice, and suddenly that was being silenced. As a result of this experience I became guarded in my writing at school. While I still wrote poetry to work through everything, I didn't share it with my teacher anymore.

This was another moment in my life when I was grateful for

my mom's strength. That afternoon, I told my parents about being called to the counselor's office. I struggled with how to cope if my writing was going to be judged as inappropriate.

"Natalie, I know writing poetry helps you process. There's a lot going on right now and you find comfort in sharing your thoughts and feelings through words. I get that." She hugged me. "Just continue to share with me, okay? Even if you can't share at school."

"Okay, I promise," I paused before continuing. "Mom …"

"Yes, Natalie?"

"You know I'm not really like him, right? I don't want to hurt myself or anyone else." I started to cry. My mom hugged me again, tighter.

"Oh, honey, I know that," she consoled me. "You're just trying to figure things out. Besides, I know you're doing okay as long as you're willing to share your poetry with me. For the record, I like our open and honest conversations about your work. It lets me know what's going on in that head of yours." I was grateful my mom understood and trusted me to deal with my emotions the way that worked best for me.

&

I was concerned about starting the ninth grade. Since the few friends I'd made were a year older than me, the next year they went on to high school. I was stuck in junior high, friendless once again. I continued to bounce between groups. Fortunately, since I was on the accelerated path for English and math, sang in the choir, and played volleyball I knew people in a wide variety of groups: nerds, choir geeks, and jocks. As a result, I got along well with most classmates and found I could float between groups. While these students were more acquaintances than friends, I at least had people with whom I could eat lunch and spend breaks.

Later in junior high, it became apparent Brenda had told some people at school about my family. A girl in one of my classes started bullying me. She would call me names, make fun of my weight, and whisper homophobic slurs. While she normally approached me when I was alone, I was always terrified she would say something loud enough for others to hear and publicly out my family. For months, I was tormented by this fear and couldn't understand why she was harassing me. I hadn't done anything to her and kept wishing she would just leave me alone. Then one day my family came to a school function.

I had already told Jerry about how she was bothering me, so that night I pointed my classmate out to him. Later when we got home he told me that he wasn't surprised she was bullying me. He told me, "I think she's a lesbian."

"How can you tell?" I asked.

"It's just a feeling I have."

"Well, if she's a lesbian, she of all people shouldn't be mean to me!"

"She's scared, Natalie. She's probably struggling to find herself and terrified people will find out. Look at how her friends have treated you. She's probably terrified they'll reject her if they find out. I know it's not easy for you and I'm not saying it's right, but sometimes people in this situation react out of fear and become hateful toward others."

I was angry. I couldn't believe that out of everyone at school, the one person treating me the worst was likely part of the LGBTQ community. Part of me desperately wanted to out her. She wouldn't have to worry so much about making fun of others in order to look straight if everyone knew she was a lesbian. I angrily shared this with Jerry. "I know it's hard and it's not fair," he responded. "No, she shouldn't treat you like this, but people need to be able to come out on their own terms. We've been lucky in so many ways. Your parents stayed friends, your mom is understanding, both your dad's family and mine were supportive. But so many people don't have that. What if her parents are like your mom's dad? What if they disowned her or kicked her out? She needs to be able to come to terms with her sexuality in her own time, and she needs to come out to friends and family when she's ready. I know it's hard to understand, especially when you're getting a raw deal, but you should never out anyone, Natalie. When someone comes out, it should always be up to that individual."

While I didn't like it and agreed I was getting a raw deal, I understood what Jerry was telling me. I thought about my own family; I couldn't imagine how different our lives would be if someone outed my dad when he was younger before he'd accepted who he was. This conversation with Jerry always stuck with me, and I never said anything about her sexuality. She continued to be rude to me for the rest of the year, but thankfully, we didn't end up at the same high school.

I haven't spoken to her since and don't know if she ever came to terms with her sexuality, but I managed to get over my anger after talking with Jerry. For the rest of that year I felt sorry for her. While I knew my dad struggled, I was never a part of his journey to accept his sexuality. I was brought in afterward, once he was ready to come out to us. This was one of the first times in my life I'd met someone early on in their quest to find their identity, the first time I met someone still conflicted and not yet ready to come out. I was saddened by her fear but reminded of how fortunate I was to have such a loving and accepting family. I couldn't imagine the feeling of worrying my parents wouldn't love me. After that, every time she would say something rude, I wanted to tell her that it was okay, that it would get better, but I also knew if she wasn't ready to acknowledge her sexuality, I couldn't be the one to bring it up. It's been almost twenty years, but I still think about her occasionally. If Jerry was right, I hope she was eventually able to come out and that her family accepted her. I hope that after all these years, she's no longer living in fear and has found happiness in her life.

I spent most of ninth grade thinking I would go back to the outcast group once I hit high school. There had been a big restructure and division of schools that year as they opened a new high school. As a smaller city where families have gone to the same school for generations, this caused quite a stir. Many people didn't like where the lines were drawn. Some challenged the boundaries so they could follow their sports coach or choir director. By the time I hit high school, the landscape had changed.

∽

Fortunately, things did get better in high school. I stayed in contact with a few friends from the outcast group, but I wasn't as close to them anymore. We'd grown apart over the past year at separate schools and things didn't feel the same. As a sophomore, I started to find myself. I stopped taking piano lessons and singing in the choir. My sister was more musical, and these were the things I did because as the younger child I had followed in her footsteps.

I focused my electives on writing and photography and took art classes after school. I also joined the Key Club and got my first dose of volunteer organizations. I fell in love with the idea I could help other people and how volunteering as a group we would increase the amount of good we could do.

This was also the year I met Liv. She was a mysterious new girl. She was edgy and attractive and had just the right amount of attitude. Starting high school can be tough for a new kid, and I knew how hard it could be to not have any friends. When I saw her sitting by herself in the hallway on her first day, I went up and introduced myself. "Hey there," I started. "I noticed that you're new and I just wanted to say hi. I'm Natalie."

"Liv," she said as she slowly eyed me up and down. "Have a seat," she said after a short pause. We started talking. She was the first person in a long time that I truly clicked with.

I found I could be honest with Liv. We had a risky but eventually trusting relationship. She had a difficult family story and, while I won't share the details of her personal life as I promised to always keep her confidence, I will say my life of secrets and isolation seemed small and insignificant in comparison.

I think part of the reason Liv and I got along so well was because we were both hiding in one way or another. She was trying to escape certain situations in her life and would sometimes lie about her past. I was living a life of secrets while I hid parts of my family in the shadows. Meeting Liv was one of the best things that could have happened to me at that point in my life. For the first time since I'd moved to Boise, I had finally found my true fit, and I finally had someone to confide in. Liv had already seen so much in her young life that my dads' sexuality wasn't very outlandish to her. While she was sensitive to the difficult situation of living in a place that wasn't accepting of homosexuality, and the intense secrecy due to my dad's position as a judge, she had no judgment. Again, living a life that most don't understand and having the strength to defy the odds often gives people a different perspective and an openness when it comes to dealing with differences.

I was in high school when they started a Gay-Straight Alliance (GSA). The goal of the GSA was to create a safe space for LGBTQ youth and allies to meet and talk about issues related to them. It felt progressive at the time. I attended a few meetings and, while it was nice to encounter people who were open-minded, I still struggled. I didn't know anyone well, so I never told them about my family. I played the role of an ally, but even as a teenager, I was keenly aware I was much more than that. I had a gay family, and we all were living in the closet. Hiding this from the people in the GSA somehow made me feel like I wasn't really a part of it. The members would never really understand just how much I belonged as part of the LGBTQ community or how much support I needed if I couldn't be honest with them about my family.

Liv and I also started to branch out with our friendship. We became close with two other girls: Amy and Eleanor. I had known Amy since I first started junior high, but she and I never really hung out despite having a couple classes together. As we became closer during my junior year, I finally confided in her as well. I was very nervous after my experience in the seventh grade, but Liv's positive reaction helped give me courage. After years of hiding my family and lying about Jerry's role in my life, I had two friends I could finally invite to my dads' home.

Before meeting Liv, I had never had a friend over to my dads' house. If people wanted to study together or hang out, I would either go to their house or we would go to my mom's place. The first time I invited Liv and Amy over was a huge milestone, not only for me but for my dads as well.

They arrived together at our house, and when the doorbell rang, my dads excitedly followed me to the door. I invited my friends in, and my dads could barely make it through my introductions before, in true Perry fashion, they skipped the handshake and threw their arms around my friends in a huge bear hug, "Welcome to our home! We're so happy to have you here!"

Before dinner, I gave Liv and Amy a tour. As we went room to room, they asked questions about family decorations like the pink triangle that hung on the wall in the entryway, and they browsed our coffee table books *Men Together* and *Stonewall*.

After dinner, we sat down to watch the current episode of *Will & Grace*. The show had quickly become a family favorite as one of the first on TV to have gay main characters. While the flamboyant Jack often stole scenes, the show also focused on a more reserved lawyer, Will, who reminded me of my dad. A few minutes in when the phrase "Just Jack!" was said, my dad and I immediately followed by shouting, "Just Jerry!" Liv and Amy both looked a little startled before they burst out laughing. "A little family joke," I told them.

As comforting as it was for me to finally have people in my life who were true friends, it was also comforting for my dads. I think my dad especially had some guilt over the years that my sister's and my friendships suffered because of the secrets in our family. However, I never felt that it was his responsibility or fault. He never chose to live in a world that would put restrictions on what a family could be or that would decide what line of work he could do based on who he loved.

❧

During high school, my strength as a person began to grow again as I started to figure out who I was. My junior year, I became the president of the Key Club, which was my first taste of program development. My desire to travel started to grow, as did my interest in experiencing a more open environment.

When I was a sophomore, I decided that I wanted to go to Spain for spring break the following year. It would be my first international trip and at $2,000, not a cheap one. I talked to my parents about it, and they told me that if I could pay for it, I could go. That summer I picked up extra shifts working at Kmart and skimped on activities and gas so that I could save. By the time I left, I'd paid the fees and had enough spending money for our eight-day trip.

During the trip, we were supposed to stick together; we were never supposed to go off by ourselves. One day I was hanging out with some of the parent chaperones who had a bit of a negative attitude, and I just couldn't handle their complaining anymore. We were in Spain! I wanted to eat good food, explore foreign places, and meet went shopping together when my dad put a box of tampons in the shopping cart.

"Darrel, we can't buy those!"

"Jerry, if they're on the list, we buy them … the girls need them. Welcome to life with teenage daughters."

When they got home from the store, this led to an entertaining conversation. "Okay, Natalie, if I'm going to be a dad I suppose I need to learn these things. I have to say I'm totally confused. What are *wings* and why do girls need them?" Katie and I then explained the difference between pads, panty liners, and tampons, applicator versus non-applicator and why there are different sizes. By the end of the conversation Jerry had decided it was hard to be a woman.

His understanding of feminine hygiene products came in handy though. Months after this educational conversation we were playing Taboo with another gay couple and their two sons. I got the word *pad* and couldn't say words like "writing" or "pen" so I yelled, "They have wings."

The other family sat at the table with blank expressions, as everyone in my family shouted, "Pads!" in unison and then burst out laughing.

Jerry was further convinced of the struggle of being a woman a couple of years later. My dad and Jerry had joined a local LGBTQ couples group and had made many friends. Every Halloween they attended a private costume party. While they've had several memorable costumes, one of my favorites was when they decided to dress up as Sonny and Cher. My dad is five feet three, so he dressed as Sonny. Jerry has a foot on him, standing at six feet three, so he dressed as Cher.

Jerry had to go shopping to find a dress. He also bought a long black wig, pantyhose, shoes, and fake nails. Katie and I supplied the makeup. The night of the party, my sister and I went over to spend a couple of hours helping him get ready. Once dressed, he put on his new people. In exasperation, I snuck off by myself. I was in Barcelona, but didn't know where exactly in the city. I wasn't even sure how to get back to our hotel. I spent the afternoon walking around seeing the sights and then tried to get a taxi. I managed to hail the cab, but when I gave him the name of the hotel, he refused to take me. Preferring Catalan, he also declined to speak to me in Spanish, so while I understood he was telling me no, I didn't understand why.

At that point I decided to just keep walking until I found someone else to ask, someone who would be patient with my broken Spanish. It only took a few minutes for me to find a police officer who spoke English. When I asked directions and explained the cab situation he chuckled and explained I was very close to my hotel and the cab wouldn't take me because it wasn't enough of a fare.

I returned to the hotel feeling like a champion. I'd just spent a day by myself walking around a city where I didn't know anyone and only *kind of* spoke the language. I was starting to think about college and knew I wanted to leave the state, but I was also nervous about what it would be like to go off on my own. As I got ready for dinner in the hotel that evening, I knew without a doubt my days in Idaho were numbered.

❧

Before I even started exploring specific colleges, I began looking at scholarship options. Because I wanted to leave Idaho, I knew I would need financial assistance to help pay for school. I was so excited when I found a scholarship for the LGBTQ community. It included allies and kids with gay parents. I knew with my story I could write an incredible essay and would have a great shot at getting the scholarship.

My elation died down when I read the small print. Winners had to be willing to have their name published, and their essay could possibly be shared outside the scholarship organization. I took the information to my dad to review, although I knew what he would say. As he finished reading, he gave me a sad look, "I'm sorry Natalie, but you can't apply for this. If you win and they publish your name or share your essay, I could be publicly outed. There's just too much unnecessary risk. You know we have to be really careful here. There will be other scholarships you'll qualify for."

I had never expected to find a scholarship I could apply for as the daughter of gay dads. I knew college would be expensive, especially out of state, and the application process can be very competitive. Generally, people apply for everything available to them. I was so angry I couldn't even apply for a scholarship I qualified for because I had to hide my family. I was also temporarily angry with the LGBTQ organizations and people who weren't more cognizant of those who live in the closeted part of their community.

My senior year was a blur. I took five advanced placement (AP) classes and worked as much as I could to save money for college. Then in October, Hurricane Iris hit Belize. Our school had taken a group of students down the previous year, and Liv and Eleanor had both gone. The town where they stayed had been hit and the devastation was horrendous.

Our friends wanted to do something but weren't sure what. Our school started collecting donations of clothes, blankets, and other emergency items to ship down. While Amy and I hadn't gone on the trip, we wanted to help our friends. Over the next several months, the four of us hatched a plan to hold the Belize Benefits Concert.

By the spring, everything was ready. The Big Easy in downtown Boise donated their concert venue, and the staff donated their time. Local musicians, such as Marcus Eaton, offered their talent free of charge. It was an amazing event, and by the end of the night we'd raised over $3,000 to donate.

By the end of my senior year, I felt accomplished: I'd taken all the classes I wanted, excelled in school, volunteered and had given back to the community, and was accepted into college. While my high school years had been good because I finally had a couple of amazing friends who accepted my family, I was ready to leave the state. Idaho overall was too small and too close-minded for me. After six years of living in a closeted family in a judgmental society, I was ready for a completely different experience.

Before I headed off to college, I had one more summer of work at Kmart. One day, I happened to be sitting in the café eating during my break when Brenda walked into the store. I hadn't seen her in a couple of years. My dads had moved to another neighborhood, and we'd wound up at different high schools with the boundary changes.

When I first saw her, I reverted back to that little girl in the seventh grade and quickly glanced away hoping she wouldn't see me. I only had a few weeks before I was leaving Idaho to attend college in New York and just wanted to escape another conversation with her. My heart sank when a shadow fell over my table and I heard her say, "Hey, Natalie."

"Hi," I forced myself to say as I looked up.

"I just wanted to say I'm sorry for, well, for everything. I know I treated you really badly and it wasn't right. I've felt bad for years for refusing to be your friend after you told me about your family. I know it's no excuse, but my parents just really weren't okay with it. But I still could've been better. I could've been nice to you at school at least. I just feel really terrible about it all and wanted to apologize. I won't be surprised if you don't forgive me, but I just needed to tell you that."

At that point, it was all I could do to fight back my tears. "Thank you. That means a lot to me. Really," I managed to say.

"Well, I have to go. Good luck with college," and with that she turned and walked out of my life. I haven't seen her since.

It takes a lot of courage for people to admit when they've made a mistake or have treated someone unfairly. I don't know when Brenda realized she didn't agree with her parents' stance. I can only imagine how difficult it was for her as a Mormon growing up in a family that was teaching her ideals that at some point she felt were wrong. While I never blamed her, because I knew she was only acting on her parents' wishes, her apology meant the world to me.

Her actions showed me that people can change. It may take days, months, or even years, but people do have control over who they become in the future. Brenda's apology was a turning point in my life.

Nothing Wrong

Write what you think and feel
That's what teachers always say
Write what's on your mind
Be truthful to yourself
So I sit and I write my feelings
I'm honest
I tell my life story
I share my pain and fears
And all you can say is
That you don't understand
That it's not right for me
To feel that way
And if I stop writing sadness
You say I'm cured
Like a doctor
I'm not sick anymore
But what you don't see
Is that I was never ill
There was nothing wrong with me
I was coping;
Dealing with life
I wasn't depressed
I wasn't suicidal
I wasn't dead
My soul's always been alive
Always been working

I've always been "alright"
Now that you accept me
Doesn't mean you see me
Doesn't mean I'll call you friend
Because if you don't understand who I was
You'll never truly begin to see
Who I am now

4 Losing Faith

After my grandfather disowned me, I lost my friends, and we weren't welcome in our church anymore due to my dad's sexuality, I had a few other negative experiences with religion. My dad found another Presbyterian church in town that accepted homosexuals in the congregation. My mom, however, struggled to find another place of worship. Because there weren't any other Presbyterian churches, we looked around at other denominations. I was intrigued by looking at other options. Presbyterian churches are quiet and reserved. Attendees go, sit down, and listen. There isn't much communication outside of a designated greeting time or much audience participation in the sermon. We had visited other churches to attend Christmas concerts and other special events and were fascinated when people would cry out "Hallelujah!" or "Amen!" The outpouring was so different from what we were accustomed to. Some of our favorite services were at a Baptist church in another neighborhood, so we found a similar church on our side of town and decided to check it out.

Everything went fine at first. We went to sermons and attended Sunday school. Katie even sang during the services on occasion. One day after church, we climbed in the car and my mom asked us how our day went. Katie and I immediately burst into tears.

Because of our three-year age difference, we were in different classes for Sunday school, but the messages had been the same. They were discussing sin and what social actions were or were not acceptable to the church.

"Abortion is a sin," they started. "Of course, you shouldn't have sex before marriage, that's a sin too. But if you somehow become pregnant, you can never get an abortion. It's murder."

A girl in my class raised her hand, "Um, if you're really young and get pregnant, what if you can't take care of a baby?"

Our Sunday school teacher looked disapprovingly at her, "Then you shouldn't get pregnant. Are there any other questions?"

The same girl raised her hand again, "What if the mom's life is in danger? Or what if you don't choose to get pregnant? Like, if a girl is raped. Or what if—?"

"There is absolutely no situation where abortion is ever acceptable. It is always wrong. If you have an abortion, God will never forgive you and you will wind up in hell. Period."

As the conversation abruptly ended, the girl shrunk in her seat. Sadly, this wasn't a foreign experience for me; I had seen this attitude before. We had to believe their way and there was no room for discussion. Next on the sin list was homosexuality. Of course, that was also wrong. I didn't dare speak up. Not only was my dad not publicly out, but I had just seen how the conversation would go. So for twenty minutes I sat there and listened to the Sunday school teacher tell me homosexuality was a sin and my dads were going to hell.

When Katie and I told our mom what had been said, she promised us we would never go back to that church. My sister was supposed to sing the following weekend. My mom called and explained that Katie couldn't sing because we wouldn't be returning. When they inquired as to why we wouldn't be returning, my mother gracefully told them we just didn't think it was the best fit for our family.

My mom is one of the strongest people I know, and I'm so lucky to have her in my life. She's always been an incredible role model who believes in doing what is right even when it is difficult. A couple of years later, my grandfather reached out before my sister's graduation. After not speaking to us for three years, he said he wanted to come but refused to do any activities with the entire family, sit with us at graduation, or go to my dads' home. My mom originally wanted her dad to come, but Katie told her that she didn't want him to be there unless he could put aside his feelings and do everything with the whole family.

This was a challenging situation for my mom. Her parents had gone to every other grandchild's graduation. But Katie was firm; she didn't want them there if that was how they were going to behave. She didn't want any negativity or discrimination during what should be a joyous celebration.

My mom listened to Katie's concerns and stepped up again to her dad. She told him if he couldn't come to support Katie and participate in the family activities then it would be better if he didn't attend. His response was to send a check for twenty-five dollars and a letter several pages long to Katie, explaining that now that she was an adult and moving out on her own, she could make her own decisions. He outlined all his beliefs about homosexuality and asked her to see God's truth.

My sister didn't want to upset our family, so she threw out the letter without telling anyone about it. My mom saw it when taking out the trash and read it. She was furious. She called her dad and had a long conversation about how unacceptable his behavior had been, but he refused to listen. Their relationship was further strained for years after.

I was in my twenties when he reached out to my mom again after being diagnosed with cancer. He said he wanted to make amends. My mom agreed to put aside their differences and try to move on. After conversations with her dad, my mom came to Katie and me and asked us how we felt about her trying to repair their relationship. We told her we thought she should do what felt right. Then she asked if we would want to speak to him.

"He hasn't asked yet about talking to you both," she said. "I just wanted to mention it to you two and see if you've ever thought about that and how you'd feel."

Katie had little interest. As an introvert, she didn't say much at the time because she needed time to process. However, her silence and reluctance was also a sign of discomfort. As she closed herself off from the conversation it was evident she didn't have much to say because she also didn't want much to do with him. She'd been hurt by being on the receiving end of his criticism when she turned eighteen. She was also still angry about his inability to love unconditionally, which is what we'd been told to believe was the teaching of God. I was on the fence.

"I'm not sure," I told my mom. "On the one hand, I do believe people can change and I would hate not to give him another chance if he truly has changed. On the other hand, I don't believe in lip service. He can't simply say he's changed. He has to be willing to show he's truly sorry and wants to make amends. He has to be sincere and apologize; he has to be strong enough to admit he was wrong all these years. I'm not interested if he's only going to meet halfway. He walked out on us and has to own that decision and realize he didn't practice God's love that he often preaches. Mistakes were made but if he's not willing to truly acknowledge they were his then I'm not going to waste my time. But if he can do all that, then I would be willing to talk to him."

My mom continued her conversations, but when they would talk on the phone, he would always bring up my dad's sexuality and question her Christianity. After that she tried writing him letters, hopeful he could honor their previous decision to agree to disagree, but his judgment always crept into his writing too. My mom never came to me again about trying to repair my relationship with him. I think in the end it was too difficult for him to take ownership of everything he'd done.

After these negative experiences with religion, I started to question whether I really believed in something that could produce so much hate. I was in junior high when I began to question my faith. As I bounced between churches with my mom or sat through Presbyterian sermons with my dad, I started to wonder if what they said was true.

"You're a sinner. Jesus died for you."

Every week I went I was told that no matter what I did, it wasn't enough. I was always making mistakes in the eyes of God and always would. In the eyes of the church, having gay dads was a sin. My family's existence was an abomination and somehow we were *less than*. In the eyes of some, I was going to hell for merely loving my parents. After a few years of hearing the same messages at various churches, I became really angry. Why wasn't I enough? Why didn't my family matter? Who was this pastor to tell me what was right and what was wrong? Why did I need a religion to guide my life?

I delved deeper into my writing. Once again, I looked to poetry to help me through internal struggles. For more than a year, I silently questioned what I believed. I didn't even share my conflicting feelings with my family, which was the first time I'd hidden my poetry. Since both of my parents were Christian, I didn't know how they'd react, and I didn't feel I could share my feelings until I had resolved my confusion and unease. I needed to figure out what I truly believed for myself without their influence.

※

By this time, I was in high school and taking another writing class. It wasn't my first time with Mrs. Thomas. She'd been the teacher for other English and writing classes I'd taken. She was one of the few teachers I'd confide in about my dads. She was familiar with my poetry and honest writing style. One day she pulled me aside. "Natalie, I want to talk to you about your poetry. I'm a little concerned as I've noticed a big shift in tone. It's become a little bitter. You know, I always support your writing and I'm not judging the content. I just felt that maybe you're going through a difficult time, so I wanted to check in with you. Is there anything you'd like to talk about?"

"To be honest, I am struggling. I'm questioning my faith. My family has faced a lot of negativity by people who claim to be Christians. It's not just my grandfather and church. Every time I turn on the TV or watch the news there's another politician saying I should be damaged because I have gay dads. They say these things in the name of God and I don't know if I can believe in a God that would teach these things," I explained.

"It sounds like you're having some conflicting thoughts then. I know your poetry helps you cope."

"Yeah, it does. I know my poetry has been dark and angry, but I'm doing okay. I just need more time to deal with all of this."

"I understand, Natalie. I'll continue to give you space here and the freedom to express yourself. Keep writing until you find what you're looking for, but also know I'm always here if you want to talk more."

❧

When I was younger, I was sure one day I would publish a book of poetry, but now when I go back, reading it pains me. Re-reading it has reminded me how resentful and hurt I was during those years as a result of the discrimination and hate I encountered at the hands of the church.

My anger toward religion did affect some of my relationships. In high school when I befriended Eleanor, I was never able to fully trust her or let her into my life. She had gone down the wrong path, getting caught up with drugs and alcohol, until she found God. When we became friends, she had just become a born-again Christian. I would be lying if I said I didn't harbor some negative feelings toward her at the time. She reminded me of my grandfather. It wasn't a fair comparison. She was never unkind to me or treated my family with disrespect. But she talked about her religion and love of God a lot when I was struggling with my own loss of faith.

Eleanor never tried to convert me or our friends. She was simply excited about her relationship with Christ. Religion was new to her, and she was in love with her newfound faith and wanted to share this with others. It's funny, because when I think of our relationship I'm reminded of something my dad heard from a pastor friend of his that described my feelings at the time perfectly, "The worst thing for organized religion is someone who just found God. They're so enamored by their newfound faith and grateful for being saved that they want everyone else to experience this feeling too. Unfortunately, their enthusiasm is often overbearing for those around them and can actually have the opposite affect by pushing people away from religion."

୬ଓ

I was sixteen when I concluded I wasn't a Christian. I still didn't classify myself as an atheist because I wasn't sure if I believed in God, but I decided I didn't believe in the church or the Bible.

The only thing left for me to do was tell my parents.

I was much more concerned about telling my mom than my dad. Of the two, I've always thought of her as more religious. I'm not sure why since both my parents went to church and prayed on a regular basis. But my mom was more vocal about her religion, signing her cards and notes to us kids with "all my love, kisses, hugs and prayers" and telling us she'd pray for us anytime we were going through a challenging time.

I told my parents I needed to meet with the two of them. We met in my mom's living room and had a long conversation. "Mom, Dad, I love you both and respect you and the way you've raised me," I started. "But there's something I have to tell you." I paused to catch my breath. "I know your faith is important to you and it's been a big part of your lives and has helped provide guidance and comfort during difficult times." I was barely holding back tears. "But I've come to realize I don't share your beliefs. I'm not a Christian."

There was a moment of silence while that sunk in. Before they could say anything, I handed them a piece of paper. "Here, I wrote this poem as I was trying to figure out how to tell you. Please read it. It may help answer some of your questions."

There was another pause as they read "Mother." The pounding of my heart broke the silence. When they finished, tears brimmed in their eyes, "Natalie, we will always love and accept you no matter who you are or what you believe."

They still had a lot of questions, and we spent a couple of hours talking. By the end of our conversation they still wanted me to look at other options. They were hopeful maybe I just hadn't found the right fit yet. I told them it wouldn't make a difference, but they were persistent I continue my search, even if that meant looking at other religions. I finally agreed but mostly because I didn't have much of a choice. I was a teenager and still living under their roof, and they had the expectation I would go somewhere on Sunday mornings.

Even though they insisted I research other religions, the church going became less and less frequent after this conversation. Katie was in college at that point, so I was the only one left at home. I think it became more of a chore for them. I could be pretty stubborn once I made up my mind, and I think they realized that forcing me to go to church wouldn't sway my opinion.

I was surprised my dad initially seemed to have a more difficult time with my lack of faith. In retrospect, I probably should have expected this as he usually needed a bit more time to adjust to change. But also, I think his own religious struggles may have had an impact on his reaction. Being raised Catholic, he had to come to terms with his own religious beliefs as a gay man. Despite his initial reservations, both of my parents were ultimately supportive, even though I know they both still wish I was a Christian.

Years later while living in Los Angeles, I had a conversation with two of my mom's siblings, my Aunt Jenn and Uncle Mark, when the three of us were spending Thanksgiving together. For the first time, Jenn asked about my religion. She's a devout Christian and has participated in several missions through her church. She has never agreed with homosexuality and has always thought of it as a sin. However, she has never believed in judging people. She's of the mindset that people's sexual orientation and lifestyle are between them and God and that He will make the final decision about that person's eternal life when they pass. As a result, she has never been rude or disrespectful toward my family. She has always loved my dad and treated him the same as she did before he came out.

At the time, we were sitting in my uncle's living room, and Aunt Jenn and I were splitting a bottle of wine after dinner. She shifted uncomfortably in her seat and cleared her throat. "Natalie, can I ask you a couple questions, specifically about your faith or rather, lack thereof?"

"Sure," I nodded as I tensed slightly. I wasn't really sure how well this conversation was going to go.

"My biggest fear has always been that you would lose your faith and turn your back on Christ because others turned their back on you and your family in God's name."

I sighed and half-smiled, "That's more or less exactly what happened." I went on to explain in detail my experiences at different churches and being turned away from people and relationships. I talked a lot about her dad, my grandfather, and how he refused to talk to us. I told her how he had said he wanted to come to Katie's graduation but refused to be in the same room with my dads, how we realized later through his letter that him wanting to come to Katie's graduation was really just a ploy to try to change our minds about homosexuality.

My aunt had tears streaming down her cheeks as I spoke, "I'm so sorry. I had no idea what you were going through. Your mom never told me those stories about our dad. I knew her relationship with him suffered, but I didn't know why. I should've been there more for you and your family." It didn't surprise me that my mom hadn't shared details with her siblings. It was hard enough for her to have a strained relationship with her dad, and she didn't want to pass this information along to her brothers and sisters and have it affect their relationships with him.

"It's okay. To be honest, I've always been grateful for you and your attitude. So many people can't accept what's different from themselves and their own beliefs. I know you don't agree with homosexuality and think it's a sin, but you've never let that affect our relationship. You still visit, you spend time with my entire family, including my dads. You never exclude them and you still love them. You're one of the few people in my life who doesn't agree with their lifestyle but still accepts them. It's always meant a lot to me."

With that, she wrapped me in the biggest hug she's ever given me and held me for a few minutes as we both cried. "Well, I guess we should pull ourselves together. It's Thanksgiving after all!" she declared and went to refill her wine.

Uncle Mark was surprised by our conversation. He had recently found God after working through some of his own struggles. Finding religion helped him work through his demons and get back on his feet again. As a result, he often related being a Christian to being a good person. He told me once, "You seem like a good Christian woman." That was his way of noting I'm a decent human being.

In our society having a moral compass is often equated with Christianity, but morals form in different ways. Religion and attending church is often where people learn right and wrong, but not always. I'm a good person because I was raised by good parents. They taught me how to care for other people, how to live in a world with empathy and compassion, how to recognize my privilege, and how to give back to those less privileged. All of these things are values I still hold dear. And while some of these principles may be viewed in some circles as Christian, a person doesn't have to be a Christian in order to be upstanding. It's completely possible to live an honorable and just life without following the rules of a religious institution.

As I write this, I'm still not religious. I got over my anger in my early twenties. It helped me a lot to move to New York and study anthropology. I took several classes, including religion. Through reading the Torah, parts of the Quran, and studying multiple religions across the world I came to learn that religion is like anything else. It can be good or bad depending on how people use it. With this understanding came a respect for religion. While I'm not a Christian or part of any other faith, I think people should have the freedom to believe what feels right in their hearts. However, I don't agree with any person who tries to use their faith to spread hateful rhetoric. I now know this is a representation of that individual person and not their faith as a whole.

Do I believe in God? I'm still not always one hundred percent sure, but most days I lean toward no. I still don't self-identify as an atheist. This has a lot to do with how atheism is perceived. Generally, people view atheists as religion ridiculers. While that may be true for some, it's not true of everyone who identifies with this group, and it's certainly not how I've chosen to live my life.

My sister and I have had in-depth conversations about this topic. She likes to play devil's advocate and says just because I don't use the word *atheist* doesn't mean I'm not one. And there's some truth to that. Of all the religions or groups I've studied, my beliefs most closely align with atheism.

For a couple of years, while living in Los Angeles, I changed my diet. I'd gone to WorldFest and learned a lot about veganism. I told people I followed a plant-based diet, but I never identified myself as a vegan for several reasons. The most basic was my reasoning and values were generally different from most vegans. I feel the same way about my religion.

In society, we have this need to categorize people and fit them into boxes. The problem is there will always be people who don't fit into these boxes. I don't think my views about religion make me special and probably many others feel similarly. While I may not be sure I believe in God, I also don't think believing in religion is wrong. For some people this makes it difficult to classify me.

There are many others who have difficulties self-identifying with the current boxes that exist in society. To me this is a sign we need to learn to delve deeper when getting to know people.

Mother

Mom,
I love you
But there is something
You have to do

I long for your
Approval in my life
I need you to help me
But you're causing me strife

I know you don't
Know what you are
Doing to me
You're not trying to scar

I need to be honest
I need to tell
I need you to know
I won't burn in hell

Please, just listen
Don't interrupt
Let me keep telling
These feelings I've kept

Hidden in my heart
Away from your eyes
I couldn't stand unacceptance
I can't be denied

Don't blame yourself
For what I'm about to say
And don't hate me
On this day

For it's not your fault
It's not to be blamed
It's just my decision
To not be the same

Know that I'm happy
This is my choice
For the first time
I have a voice

What I need to tell you
Christian, I am not
Don't be disappointed
It's not what you've taught

I know you base
Your standards and values
On His love
But this I can't do

I can't sit and pray
Each night
Hoping He's listening
And He'll show me the light

I don't need Him
To show me the way
For I experience it
Each and every day

I know the hate
And sense the fear
I see the crimes
That exist here

This is my world
And I can't sit by
Ignoring people and nature
Until I die

I believe people
Don't have faith
They just need to explain
Their beliefs' base

People have
This uncontrollable desire
To explain life
Which I don't admire

I don't need to know
If Jesus was His son
If the world was flooded
Or of the Garden of Eden

If there is a God
I doubt he'd want this book
To be the basis of
The beliefs people took

It's not really faith
If you believe what you're told
You need to discover for yourself
Or you'll die empty and cold

Mom,
I know you disagree
But I still can't change
I hope you'll see

Ask not
If God, I believe
I cannot answer
I can't deceive

I'm still confused
Still have more to ponder
But I needed to tell you
So you wouldn't wonder

Why I flinch
When you speak of the Bible
Why my eyes glaze over
When you say this title

Why I turn away
When you speak of his love
Of His miracles
Angels from above

I know you'll ask
What I dream
When I think of Grandpa
And all he means

Here in my life
He helped me grow
I felt his love, but
I've let him go

I believe in nature
That's where he's buried
In the earth
As if a seed

I think he's helping
Nature to grow
Helping it live
Helping it know

That when it dies
It will do the same
Be buried forever
As earth's claim

I know you do not
Understand
I know you won't lend
Me a supporting hand

I do not hate you
For your fear
So please trust me
Don't shed tears

I do not know
How people can claim
To have such faith
One and the same

Animals don't live for God
They don't think
They don't believe in Him
Or try to speak

If nature doesn't
Agree with you
How can you be angry
For my beliefs that are true

I say all of this
To let you know
I want your approval
While I grow

But if you decide
Not to let me
Live life as I choose
You're not accepting

If you decide
To think I'm wrong
To disagree
Or to scorn

And if you let these
Feelings of pain
Take over your soul
There's nothing to gain

Except the fact
That you've become
Just like your father
Whose heart is numb

I need your love
Long for approval
So please accept me
Beliefs and all

Part 2
Leaving Idaho 2002-2011

5 New York

When it came time to apply for college, all I knew was that I desperately needed to leave Idaho. After six years of hiding from everyone and lying about my family, the one quality I wanted in a college was to be somewhere, anywhere, that was the exact opposite of everything I'd always known.

My parents were supportive but also pragmatic. If I was going to apply to out of state or private schools, I needed to know what I wanted to study. They saw no sense in me paying the high out-of-state tuition to take core classes.

While I wanted to study anthropology, there weren't any classes or opportunities for high school students in my area, and I was hesitant to declare it as my major. I did know I wanted to become fluent in Spanish. My Grandma Izzy's family was from Spain. They came to the United States to work the sugar plantations in Hawaii in the early 1900s. My great grandparents only learned enough English to get by so my dad, uncles, and aunt also learned some Spanish when younger. Spanish was Izzy's first language, but she married my grandfather, a non-Spanish speaking man. As my great grandparents' generation passed on, the rest of the family stopped speaking Spanish in their homes. After a few generations, no one in my family spoke Spanish fluently. Even though Grandma Izzy grew up bilingual, she can't even understand the Spanish channel anymore when she watches it on TV.

After taking four years of Spanish in high school, I realized how much I enjoyed learning the language. I also knew how important it was to Izzy (and me) to have someone in our family revive the language, and I decided I wanted to continue learning it. I decided that if I was going to take Spanish classes for four years, I might as well get a degree. So my goal was to find a school with good Spanish and Anthropology programs in a big city on the East Coast.

I'd always been independent and, while I kept my parents in the loop, I didn't ask for their help in researching schools. However, my dad did suggest I look into Hofstra University because of a law clerk application he'd received from an applicant who'd studied there a couple of years before. Whenever he had an applicant who'd gone to school at an unfamiliar place, he would look it up online to research the institution and their law school program. He learned the school was supposed to be diverse, socially aware, and an open environment. A little extra research into the study abroad and Honors College programs caused him to make a mental note that it might be a school I would be interested in someday.

I also didn't seek academic or career advice from anyone at my high school. I knew several had a penchant for supporting local schools but was devastated when one called me into their office to discuss my plans. I explained that I'd narrowed the list of schools where I would apply and will never forget the "advice" I was given.

"Natalie, those are all out of state, private schools that are very expensive. You probably won't get in and even if you do, you won't be able to afford them."

Now I know that I can be a stubborn person, and it can be difficult for people to sway me from something when I've made up my mind, but hearing this adult, who was supposed to help guide students with sound advice, tell me I wasn't good enough was heartbreaking.

I returned home shattered. When my mom asked about my day, I burst into tears. I told her what had happened, and she hugged me.

Mom then told me I had a solid plan and should follow my heart. She knew I had a plan B. If I didn't get in, I would take a year off, work, and save money for college and reapply to schools the next year.

Some people didn't understand why I wasn't going to apply to even one in-state school. For me, the choice was simple. While growing up in a state like Idaho, a lot of teenagers dream about leaving. Some of them even apply out of state, but most end up staying. Some say they'll just do two years of core classes and then transfer, but many never do. Rural states can be hard to escape. Chances need to be taken when opportunities arise, and I knew I needed to leave. There was no way at that point in my life that I could continue to live in Idaho. I was afraid if I gave myself even a small chance of an out that somehow I'd wind up stuck in Idaho forever.

Fortunately, the advice was wrong. While I didn't get accepted to all the schools to which I applied, I did get into three of the five. One even gave me a full ride scholarship. However, that school was smaller than I'd decided I wanted, so I crossed it off my list without even visiting.

Having narrowed my choices to two colleges, the only thing left to do was visit each campus. My dad took the lead as he often did when it came to planning things. He booked the plane tickets, plus trains and hotels. I couldn't believe it when he told me the dates he had planned: we would be leaving the day before prom. At first, I was angry and upset he hadn't talked about the dates before making reservations. Senior prom is supposed to be a rite of passage. He felt guilty and even looked at changing everything, but the fees to change were so expensive it ultimately wasn't worth it. I never told him this, but later I was secretly relieved I would have a reason to miss prom. I didn't have a date yet and was nervous about whether I would be asked.

I had a great time traveling with my dad. We flew into Washington, D.C. and of the two schools we were visiting, I was leaning toward the University of Maryland in College Park. I'd heard great things about the school. They were supposed to have many international students as well as opportunities to study abroad. Since I'd decided to declare Spanish as my major, I insisted on not only doing a campus tour, but also sitting in on a class. I didn't mind that I was being a total nerd because I really cared about what kind of education I would get. I enjoyed the class I attended and the campus, but things just didn't click. The school was larger than I'd anticipated and as I walked around, I felt like I would too easily get lost in the shuffle.

I was disappointed when we left. When it comes to big decisions, I tend to be analytical and like to think things through clearly. Usually after I've done my research, I have a definite feeling of what choice is right. I had thought for sure this would be my school. I was nervous because I only had one more place to visit. I hadn't even considered what would happen if I didn't like either of my top two schools.

When we left College Park, we flew to Long Island, New York to visit Hofstra University. I immediately fell in love with the campus. It's an arboretum so the grounds are beautiful with a variety of trees. As we took our tour, we saw classes being conducted outside as students sat on the lawn. Our guide explained that teachers and students feel cooped up over the cold winter, so once spring came, it was common for some professors to teach outdoors.

After our tour, I attended a Spanish class. I remember being surprised by the small class size with only about twenty students in the room. The kind professor welcomed me and even encouraged my participation in their conversation. Afterward, I was smiling as I met my dad in the hallway. "This is where I'm going to school," I told him.

"Well, let's go back to the hotel and talk about this. You still haven't gotten your financial aid package and this is a private school. We'll need to wait and see what the numbers look like."

"Dad, I'm going to school here. I don't care about the numbers; I'll figure that part out. But this is where I'm spending the next four years," I said firmly.

My dad beamed at me, "Thank God! I didn't want to say anything, but I know University of Maryland was your first choice before we came out here. I was nervous when you didn't sound very excited after we visited. Let's hope your financial aid package is good and that you get some scholarships."

My older sister had chosen to stay in state after high school, so my choice to study in New York was a major adjustment for the whole family. We got a trial run before I headed off to college. After I graduated high school, I spent the first part of the summer studying at a bilingual school in Mexico. It gave me another chance to travel and allowed me to work on my Spanish-speaking skills before starting college.

When it came time to move to New York, my whole family saw me off at the airport. My mom and dad were going with me to help me get settled, but Jerry and Katie were staying in Idaho. I was emotional as we stood on the curb at the drop-off zone. I was crying as I hugged Jerry. "Just remember, Natalie, this is what you wanted."

I stopped and looked at him quizzically, as did the rest of the family. "Jerry, that's a terrible thing to say!" I admonished. "You're supposed to be comforting me."

"I am!" he said. "Or at least, I'm trying. You're standing here crying, like you're upset, but this *is* what you wanted. You're leaving Idaho and going to a big city."

At that, the family started laughing. He was trying to comfort me, but it just wasn't quite coming out right. On the bright side, this has now become a catchphrase for my family. Any time someone is experiencing a change in their life and is nervous or unsure about the transition, like when my dads later moved to Palm Springs, someone will always quip, "Just remember, this is what you wanted!" and everyone will break into laughter.

❧

My parents spent a couple of days in New York helping me get situated. As we carried boxes through the hall to my room, I heard Russian, Greek, and Italian being spoken amongst the families on the floor. I'd never experience so much diversity in my life. When I mentioned this to my roommate, she looked confused. "I've never been around so many white people before," she said. My eyes and mind were going to be opened a lot over the next four years.

It was an interesting time to move to New York; it had been less than a year since 9/11. While there was still some fear of future terrorist attacks, overall I found the city much more inviting than what I was accustomed to. My first semester was challenging as I still experienced some culture shock. New Yorkers can be their own breed: loud, opinionated, and walking like they're always on a mission. It was polar opposite of the slower, calmer, and quieter Northwest lifestyle I'd grown up with. And yet it only took a few months to acclimate and find myself in love with this new city.

The thing I loved about New York was that for the first time in my life, I was honest with everyone about my family. They had put together a mini-photo album for me to take to school, so I could have a piece of my family with me in New York, yet something that wouldn't take up much space in my bag as I moved my life across the country. I kept it on my desk and, when people visited my dorm, they would often flip through and ask questions. I moved to New York for openness and freedom, so I decided that from day one I was going to tell people about my dads when it came up.

I was amazed by the difference in reactions. Generally, people were a little caught off guard, but it didn't matter to them. They were surprised because there simply weren't that many visible gay families with children my age at the time, but they didn't judge me for having gay dads. They often asked questions because they were truly curious and wanted to learn more about my family structure. It was the complete opposite from Idaho where only a handful of people were accepting. In New York, only occasionally did I encounter someone who would be rude or treat me poorly because I had gay dads.

One situation does stand out in that regard. Some people think if they phrase judgment as a question, that it's not rude. A girl in my dorm once asked me with disgust in her voice, "So, your dads, like kiss, like in front of you?"

I looked at her for a minute trying to figure out if she was serious. "Do your parents ever kiss in front of you?"

"Well, yeah, but … it's different. They're straight."

"No, it's not different. Seeing my parents share a kiss when Jerry gets home from work and my dad is cooking in the kitchen isn't different from any loving straight couple that is genuinely happy to see their partner at the end of a long day at work."

I will never understand why some people feel the need to comment on things they disagree with. This girl didn't care about learning about my family. Her goal was to use a question to open a conversation so she could express how wrong she thought my situation was. I'd had enough of that negativity growing up.

During the spring of freshman year, my dads came to visit, and they wanted to meet my new friends. They bought a stack of pizzas, took it to the dorm lounge, and I invited people to stop by. They got to chat with everyone and my friends all got a free meal.

In addition to the time they spent with me on campus, we spent time together in Manhattan. We went to dinner and a show. Most of my friends were shocked when we went to go see *Naked Boys Singing* as a family. But when I think back on my time in New York, it's not the moments others found astonishing that I remember most. The one that still stands out to me is walking down the street in the Village. While strolling slightly behind my dads, I realized they were holding hands. It was the first time I'd ever seen them do so in public, and they'd been together for over six years. They seemed so happy and free.

I became even more aware of how unique my family was after I moved to New York. I only knew a handful of gay people in high school, and I only talked about my family with one of them. Yet in college, I met people with a wide range of backgrounds when it came to sexuality. I met Ben my freshman year, right when he was dealing with his own sexuality. At first, he thought he was bisexual. He'd never known anyone from a gay family, so he had a lot of questions about my upbringing. What was it like having gay dads? Did I like Jerry? Was it ever hard for me?

One day, Ben came to my room and told me he wanted to talk. "I'm gay," he said.

"I thought that might be the case."

He smiled. "It just took me awhile to accept that. I think part of the difficulty was the idea that as a gay man, I never thought having a family would be a possibility and I can't stand the idea that I would never have kids. To be honest, meeting you and your family gave me hope that even as a gay man I might have children of my own one day."

∼

After taking an anthropology class that first semester, I declared it as a second major. In retrospect, I shouldn't have hesitated. Being raised in a family that was so little understood by society, I felt a need to learn more about others. Growing up with adversity and constantly being told my family was wrong or that I was somehow damaged as a result of my family structure made me question when people said the same thing about others, whether it was regarding race, religion, gender, or relationship orientation.

In anthropology classes I felt at home. I had a lot to learn about other minorities and their history in our country. Being from a state that was ninety-three percent white and predominantly Christian, I had grown up in a sheltered environment. Being in New York gave me the opportunity to learn more about how others have dealt with their own adversity and discrimination. It also gave me the opportunity to learn, not just from classes and books, but also from my friends' personal experiences.

Moving to New York taught me to be open and honest. I slowly began to trust people again, and some of the walls I'd built over the years were slowly starting to break down. Every positive or non-negative reaction I encountered taught me even more that there were many open-minded and accepting people in the world. I stopped worrying about what people would think or how they would react. And the few people that didn't react well or were rude weren't people I needed in my life.

This was one of the beautiful things about college. In high school, we are limited to the people in school with us. In my case, I could choose to be friends with the roughly three hundred people in my class. My school wasn't big. Even the people I wasn't friends with, I still saw every day. I still heard their conversations in the hallways and still listened to their opinions in class.

One of the great things about college centered on how it was the first time I could truly choose who to surround myself with. Sure,

I ended up with people I didn't know or like in class, but I could choose roommates, where I lived, what events I attended, and who I went with. I also had made the choice to study two fields focused on diversity. Anthropology is the study of people and culture so everyone was very open-minded. I had Spanish professors from several different countries and many of the students were from different backgrounds as well.

Since Spanish and anthropology were both smaller departments filled with diverse people and ideas, I never faced discrimination in those classes. However, I sometimes felt myself challenged when coming face-to-face with new ideas or experiences people shared. I was one of three non-Hispanic students in the Spanish department, and I often realized during these discussions just how veiled my life in Idaho had been, especially when dealing with racial or ethnic minorities.

Over the years, I've heard some white people talk about how these situations can make them uncomfortable, but I don't ever remember feeling that way. Maybe because I've been a minority myself, I was more open to these situations. I never felt unwelcomed by the other minority groups I encountered. We had many conversations regarding our life experiences and the similarities and differences that existed in our worlds. I had a lot to learn, but I was always grateful for these exchanges. The goal of our conversations was always to share and educate each other.

※

My family worked hard to remain close while I was living in New York. They had created a few new family traditions when my sister had started college in Northern Idaho, and they continued those with me. My dad sent two handwritten letters every week so I would get mail. He also started sending a family email every Friday. While my mom has never been much of a letter writer, she found joy in sending a care package every month. And on Sundays I would block a few hours for our weekly phone calls.

My junior year of college, I finally met and started dating my first boyfriend. We'd been together for a couple of months when I went home for Christmas. When I was younger, my mom told me that she wanted me to wait until I was married to have sex. I've always been so independent that even as I a child, I was never sure I wanted to get married. I remember telling my mom when I was little, "I want to be a mom, but I'm not sure I want a husband." So when she told me in my teens that she wanted me to be a virgin until marriage, I told her that wasn't going to happen.

"I don't even know that I want to get married. What am I supposed to do, end up as a ninety-year-old virgin? I don't think so."

After that, our conversations about sex focused on waiting until I found someone I cared for, making sure I was comfortable taking that step and not making decisions because I felt pressured. She also told me that she would like me to talk to her when I made the choice to have sex for the first time.

I was twenty that Christmas vacation when I told her about the upcoming first time with my boyfriend. "I care about him, I'm ready and it feels right to me." It was ironic in that I hadn't even told him yet. He knew I was a virgin and had respectfully told me to just let him know if and when I was ready for that stage.

I mentioned this conversation to one of my friends. "You talked about that with your *mom*?" she asked me incredulously.

"Yeah, we talk about a lot of stuff. I know it seems weird to some people, but my family is very open. I can talk to my parents about anything." To this day, I never hesitate to talk with my family. Sometimes I may go to different people. Between my mom, dad, and Jerry, I have options of who I can share things with. It usually depends on the topic, their experiences, and what type of guidance

I'm looking for. But I never shy away from going to at least one of them when looking for advice.

After I returned to school, I did lose my virginity to my boyfriend. Our relationship ended a few months later, and I turned to my parents again for their love and support while I dealt with my first broken heart.

❧

Being an anthropology major, I knew my senior year would be devoted to learning about methodology and then conducting research for my senior thesis. I had several interests that ranged from Native Americans, race relations, and religion to Latin America. Needless to say, I was struggling to pick an area of specialization.

When it came time to choose a topic, I finally decided my focus would be sex and sexuality after taking a class titled Woman and Men in Anthropological Perspective. I'm not sure why it took me so long to realize that this was a good fit. After growing up with gay dads and witnessing society's reaction, I had a strong interest in the topic in general. Being in an environment where we could discuss all the topics that were taboo and to be open about them was also an incredibly liberating experience.

For a long time, I considered doing my thesis on gay families. There were only a few resources out at the time, and I thought it would be interesting. But I also realized that because it was an issue that hit so close to home, I couldn't be objective in researching other families. Coming from that environment myself I knew I had a huge bias and would go into it with preconceived notions. Ultimately, I decided it wasn't the right time for me to study that topic because I wanted to do my research in an area where I could be impartial.

The topic of my thesis came to me spontaneously one night when

I attended a mock gay wedding on campus. It was in support of gay rights and instead of saying wedding vows, people were listing all the rights they were denied because they weren't able to legally marry their same-sex partner.

"Legally, I'm not considered family. I'm not allowed hospital visitation when my partner is sick. If my partner is gravely ill, I'm not allowed to make end-of-life decisions for them."

"I'm not considered my child's parent because I didn't carry them in my womb. I'm not listed on their birth certificate. If my partner and I separate in the future I can be denied custody."

"We have to pay more as a family for health insurance. We have to buy separate plans because I can't be listed as their spouse."

"We can't plan for retirement as a couple. We have to have separate accounts. I can't receive my partner's retirement or social security benefits after they pass."

It was supposed to be an educational opportunity for people to learn why marriage equality is so important. I found the event fascinating, although there wasn't anything mentioned in the vows that I didn't already know. I was more intrigued that an LGBTQ event like this would be held on campus. Plus, I thought it was a great way to represent the lack of protections gay couples faced at the time.

I already knew the dangers gay couples faced. My dads had taken many measures to have documentation in place and to write wills that would legally protect them. Unfortunately, at the time, those measures were still being challenged in several courts across the country when other family members didn't agree with their relationship. I've always known I'm very fortunate to have a family who was able to discuss these decisions with each other. We all knew each other's preferences if someone became terminally ill, and we'd all agreed to respect those wishes.

It was at this event that I first heard of polyamory. An acquaintance was chatting with her friend and discussing her polyamorous lifestyle and the rights she and her poly partners were denied. I'm a naturally curious person who, in general, isn't shy about asking questions and my ears perked up when I heard their conversation.

"Hey there, I didn't mean to eavesdrop but I heard you use the term polyamory. I'm not familiar with this. Do you mind telling me a little more about it?"

"Sure," she responded. "I'm pretty open about my life and I'm here at this event to help educate. Polyamory is the idea of loving more than one person at the same time; it literally translates to *many loves*."

"Oh, okay. So you have multiple partners then. Is this a lifestyle you choose?" I asked.

"No, it's not a choice. Those who live a polyamorous lifestyle believe that the same way there's a sexual orientation, there is also a relationship orientation. While some people are born monogamous, they believe others are born polyamorous."

"How do people know they're polyamorous? I've never heard of a relationship orientation and never thought much about choices existing outside of monogamy. Do people go through a similar process like when a gay person comes out?"

She smiled. "Kind of. Most poly people realize their orientation at some point in their lives when they are in a relationship and fall in love with a second person without falling out of love with the first person they're in a relationship with. As a bisexual that realization for me was pretty similar to when I first realized I was attracted to both men and women."

We talked for over an hour because I had many more questions. I walked away with her contact information that evening; a list of resources to look into, including books and local poly groups; and the knowledge that I'd just found the topic for my thesis.

After my conversation at the mock wedding, I was eager to talk with my professor at our next class and discuss what she thought about me doing my thesis on polyamory. I was pleased she was just as excited about the topic as I was. As we looked into it, she found no other anthropological or sociological work had been written on the topic at that time. Since this would be a big endeavor, she went to the department chair and decided that instead of me doing a three-credit thesis, I would do a six-credit thesis for departmental honors.

I was surprised as I started to conduct my research. I reached out to the groups that had been suggested and all of them were willing to invite me to their monthly meetings. Because I was there for research and the group environment is meant to be a safe place for poly people, at the beginning of each discussion they would introduce me and explain that I was there for academic research. They also provided everyone the time and option to tell me if they didn't want their words to be used as part of my research.

The first couple of meetings I was apprehensive as I honestly expected to have people speak up and tell me that they were uncomfortable with me being there or didn't want to be included in my work. Growing up in a closeted gay family, I was quite used to the idea that there are people who aren't comfortable with their private information being shared. However, during the year of my fieldwork, I found that not one person came to me stating that they were uncomfortable with my presence, and actually most of them were very excited to have somebody doing anthropological research on their community.

Conducting my research was a fascinating experience and an opportunity to encounter what I can only assume some straight families feel when they first learn about my gay family. Growing up with the idea that everybody is monogamous and that is the so-called correct way, I was learning about a lifestyle that was totally different from everything I have known my entire life. I understood how challenging it could be to question what a person has always been told is right and how difficult it could be to open one's mind to something that is difficult to understand because no context for it exists in that person's life. But by the end of my research, I found poly people and their families to be just like everyone else.

There are many different family structures today. While some consist of a married husband and wife, other types of families include single-parent households, divorced parents, half-siblings, stepfamilies, gay families and yes, even polyamorous families. Ultimately, the one thing that makes a family is love. I was reminded of this during my thesis research; it didn't matter how I personally felt about polyamory, and it didn't matter if I was monogamous or polyamorous. At the end of the day, we should all be able to recognize that love is love.

Living in New York helped open my eyes to the world for the first time. Every day I heard different languages and met people from other countries. Moving there after experiencing a somewhat sheltered childhood made me realize how little I truly knew and understood about the world and different cultures. That seemingly small distance of travel across the country inspired me to travel across the world.

Ready

I want to live
I think I'm ready
To step outside
On my own
And survive
I think I can
Take that step
Trust myself
Take the dare
And not break
I think it's all right now
To try to be me
I think it's okay
To find myself
I want to live life
Solely for me
Not my mother,
Nor my father
Only I can decide
Life's big decisions
I think I have
The power now
To do so
And if I
Take this step
And fall

It will still be
All right
Because it's just
Another attempt
To succeed
In life
And the only success
That I need
Is to be me
Whoever that may be

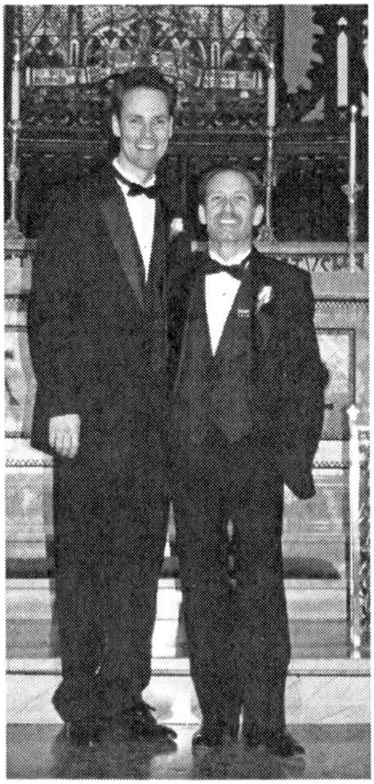
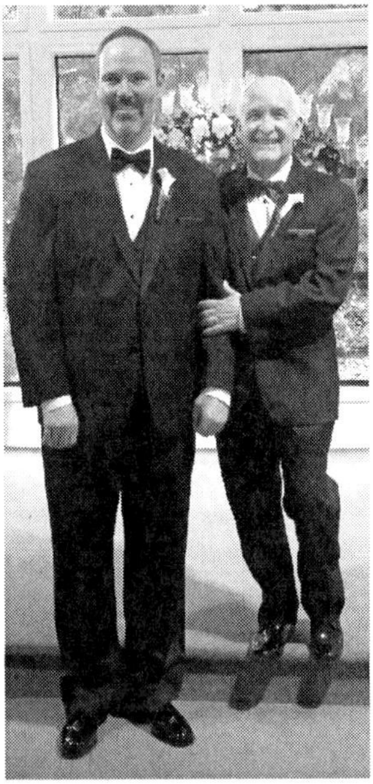
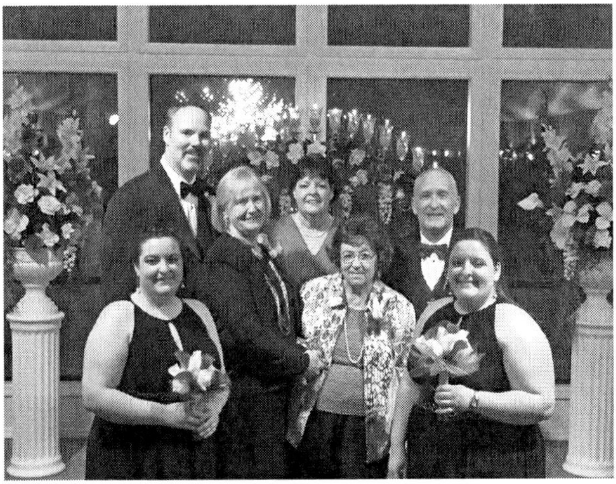

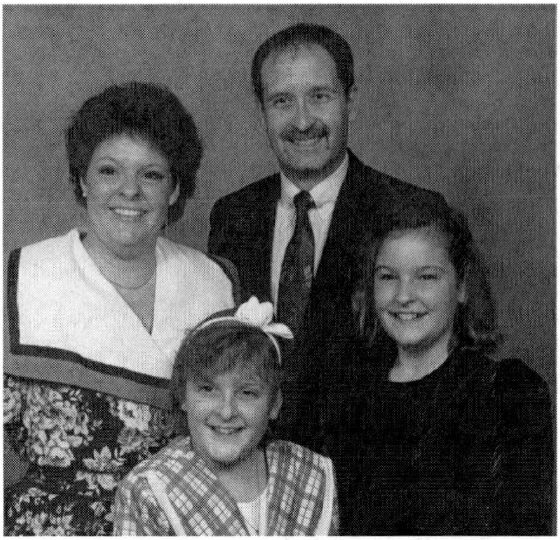

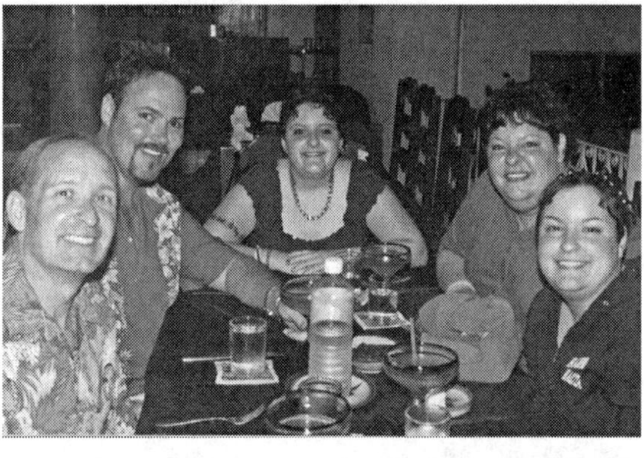

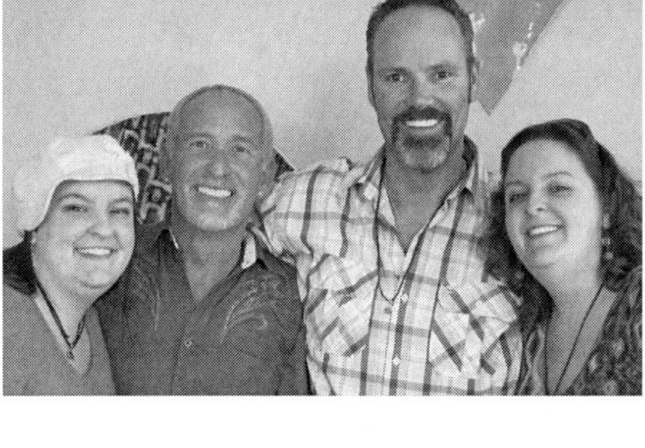

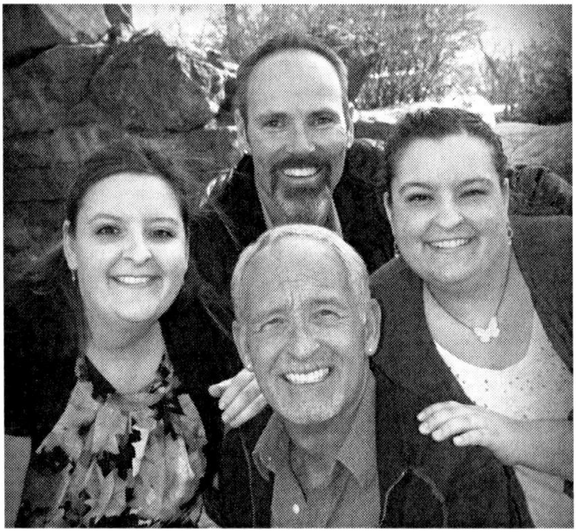

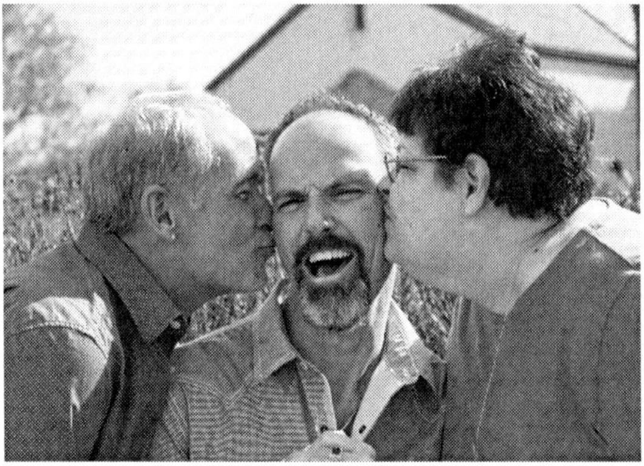

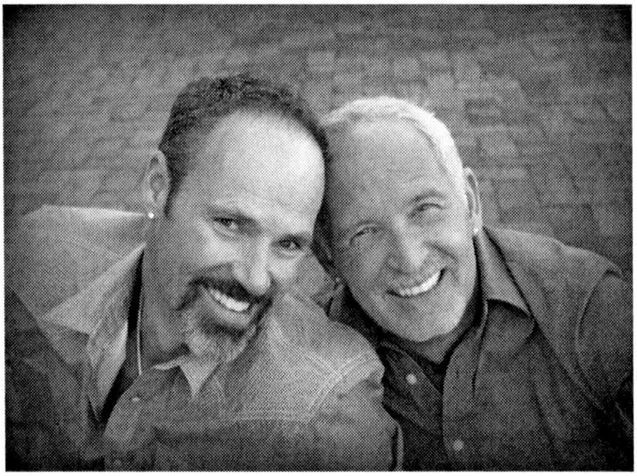

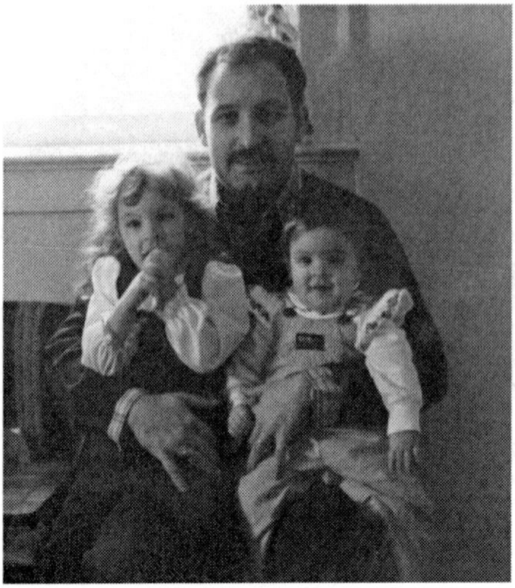

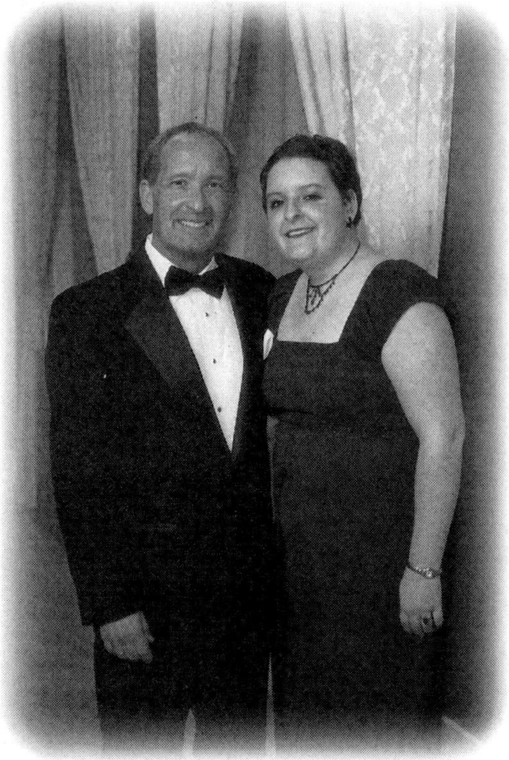

6 Europe

Toward the end of my sophomore year, I started thinking about what I would do to celebrate my college graduation. I decided I wanted to travel. That summer I started working out a plan and looking at costs. I gave myself two years to save so I would be able to backpack through Europe for three months.

During junior year, I worked hard, stuck to my budget, and was excited thinking about how great the trip would be. A few months later, an opportunity came up to study in China the following summer. It was an extensive six-week program through the Honors College and almost everything was covered: eight credits, housing, weekend excursions, a week playing in Beijing, visas, and airfare. All I had to pay was $2,000. After a long talk with my parents during which I asked for their opinions, I decided to take the money out of savings and go. I knew this would affect my budget for Europe, but in the end, I decided it was worth it.

Ten students were chosen for the scholarship, and I was able to be open with them about my family. Since it was a trip for college credit, we didn't have any other students in our classes and only got to know a few locals during evening activities and while on weekend excursions. Being there certainly fueled my hunger for travel. It was the first time being in another country when I didn't know the language and where very few people spoke English. My high school trip to Spain had highlighted my independence and readiness to leave Idaho. The trip to China made me realize I could successfully travel to parts of the world I was less familiar with. I came home confident that if I could find my way in China I would also be able to navigate my way through Europe.

I realized I wouldn't have enough saved for my backpacking trip. Since it was my last year of school and tuition had already been paid, everything I made went toward the trip. I decided to get a second part-time job and work forty hours a week during my senior year of college. By the end of the year, I had reached my goal of saving $8,000, but I encountered another challenge during the second semester.

I was supposed to travel with my friend Brandy, but she found out her cancer was no longer in remission, and she would need to start undergoing treatment again. I knew she was having some health problems and was fatigued, but she was hesitant to tell me the extent of her issues. She ended up withdrawing from some of her classes as she couldn't carry a full class load. She finally told me in the spring she wouldn't be able to travel with me.

My heart broke for her. Not only was her health not good enough to spend three months in Europe, but since she had withdrawn from classes, she wasn't able to graduate as planned. I completely understood how personal this was and her reluctance to share the severity of her illness. It was only a few months before my trip, and I knew none of my other friends would be able to save enough money in time. I had a big decision to make: Should I cancel a trip that I'd been planning for two years? Or should I bite the bullet and go by myself?

I thought about it a lot. On the one hand, I was a terrified of travelling overseas by myself for an extended period. On the other hand, this was something I'd wanted for so long and had worked so hard for that I couldn't imagine just walking away from it. In the end, I decided to go for it.

My flight left a week after classes finished. My whole family came to New York to celebrate my graduation. My parents returned to Idaho following our family celebration, while my sister spent an additional week with me in New York before I flew to Europe. We got a hostel in the city and spent the days doing all the touristy things I hadn't done in the four years I'd lived in New York. It was very busy and a lot of fun. But what I remember most about that time was the last night.

As I was packing my bag in the hostel and organizing myself for my trip, I was overcome with anxiety and broke down in tears. As I sat on the floor surrounded by my clothes and toiletries I bawled because I was terrified of the choice I'd made and convinced I was making a mistake. My sister looked at me, "Natalie, you're so strong. If anyone can do this, you can. I've always admired your courage. Most people would let their fear stop them from doing the things they want in life, but you never do. You came to New York for school and now you're headed to Europe. You're going to be just fine. And if you doubt yourself right now, trust me, because I know you got this."

Katie, whom I've thought of as my personal cheerleader ever since, helped me finish packing my bag, and the next morning I was sitting on a plane headed to Ireland. After living in New York and being so open with my friends, I felt myself challenged again. Should I tell people I would meet about my dads? It's common when traveling for new people to ask about where someone is from and how their family feels about the trip, especially as a solo female traveler. I knew Europe was supposed to be a very open place as well, but I also knew I'd be meeting people from all around the world.

I didn't know what the best approach would be, so I decided to wait until I got there and then see how comfortable I was with people. I was only spending a few days in each city and didn't want to spend all of that time trying to explain my family structure to the other travelers I met. The uncertainty of how people would react was too great to deal with, so I ultimately decided not to share details. My story went back to having divorced parents, neither of whom remarried.

I was only a few weeks into the trip when I went to Amsterdam. I spent a day visiting the Anne Frank House. Of all the sites Amsterdam has to offer, this was the most famous and one of the hardest to visit. The books and commentaries pointed out the site's current relevance. The guidebook included Anne's words from April 9, 1944: "We can never be just Dutch, or just English, or whatever, we will always be Jews as well. But then, we'll want to be."[1] Today, people are still being persecuted and murdered because they, just like Anne, are not only "different" but also are proud of their personal identity. I realized how meaningful the Anne Frank House still is, especially in relation to other groups still being discriminated against.

Personally, I believe that visiting sites such as this are incredibly difficult and absolutely necessary. We should all be reminded of the atrocities of our world's past because acknowledging and remembering such acts hopefully will influence our own attitudes and behavior in modern times.

Walking through the door of her house took my breath away. It was larger than I had anticipated but still cramped for a tour full of people. Even with having read her diary, and thinking I knew what to expect, I was still surprised at how strong my reaction was. I couldn't even make it through the first room before I had to take the tissues out of my bag. Walking through the house, knowing I was standing in the same place that these eight people stood, ate, lived, and breathed was an enlightening experience. Seeing the personal objects and displays made it seem like pieces of the inhabitants were still there. Reading portions of the diary as I journeyed through reminded me of moments that had occurred in that exact location.

As I walked into the second set of rooms, a woman in front of me was sobbing as she looked at some of the items. "Excuse me," I said. "Would you like some tissues?"

"Oh, thank you, that's very kind. I'm having a difficult time, more so than I expected."

I stood next to her as she wiped her eyes. "It's all right," I comforted her. "I don't think there's a dry eye here."

She gave me a weak smile. "My grandmother was killed in Auschwitz. I've wanted to come here for a while because it's such an important part of our history. I knew it would be very challenging." She paused as we stepped into the next room. "It's strange the mix of conflicting reactions I'm having now. I feel incredibly blessed to be here but also emotionally tortured. This house, it represents a horrible memory of the past but also a strong advisory for our future." We walked through the rest of the house in silence. By the time we reached the end, my tissues were gone.

It came as a surprise that the attic was actually three stories. When I read the diary a long time ago, I had pictured it as all one floor. I couldn't believe they could successfully hide there for years without people realizing there should be more to the warehouse when inside. The stairs were cramped and steep. I recall they creaked, which made me realize how difficult it must have been for them to walk around silently during the day when there were workers downstairs.

After finishing the tour, I too was emotionally devastated, but there was another important site I wanted to see around the corner. I thought the most sentimental part of my trip would be visiting the Anne Frank House, but I was wrong. The most profound moment was standing at the Homomonument. One of the most incredible things about the monument is that it's not something that was recently constructed in reaction to the gay rights movement of the past decade. It was unveiled in 1987. In Amsterdam, there was a call to create a memorial for the gay men and women murdered during WWII and immediately following the war. It took almost forty years of thorough research into their persecution to complete the story and for the monument to be constructed.

Many people don't know homosexuals were oppressed under Hitler's regime. They were arrested and deported to the concentration camps and gay men were forced to wear pink triangles as a symbol of their homosexuality. To make them identifiable from a distance, the triangles were two to three centimeters larger than those worn by other prisoner groups.

The Homomonument displays the statement, "Never again" to show that history shouldn't be repeated. However, it doesn't only commemorate the victims of WWII, it also represents all homosexuals who have been or still are being persecuted around the world. The beauty of the monument isn't only the symbol of the three pink granite triangles but also the message it illustrates by representing the past, present, and future. The triangle symbolizing the past was placed at ground level between the paving stones, and it points toward the Anne Frank House. This is a simple reminder of what can happen when people let hate, judgment, and intolerance rule their lives.[2]

The triangle for the present has a set of steps that leads from the street and protrudes into the canal. The point of the triangle faces the National War Memorial in the center of Amsterdam. The triangle for the future, which is raised sixty centimeters above the ground, points to COC Amsterdam, which is the world's "oldest continuously operating gay and lesbian organization."[3] For me, these two triangles remind us where we are today and how far we still have to go.

I spent an entire afternoon at the monument, eating lunch and people watching. I will never forget how totally and completely safe and accepted I felt. After my experiences in Idaho and the United

States in general, I was stunned to be in a country that not only recognized, but made a grand political statement of acceptance and tolerance by creating a monument to the gay community. I knew this was a place where I would never need to hide who my family was or fear the judgment of others. I know no country or people are perfect, but I've believed since that moment that Amsterdam has it right. We could all learn a lot about humanity and decency from the Dutch.

My time in Amsterdam was also the first time I realized my family structure affects my perception of travel. The Homomonument and the openness of the Dutch made such an impact on me because I have a gay family. The knowledge that I didn't have to fear this country or society gave me a comfort I am eternally grateful for, but I'm also aware this wouldn't have been such a profound moment if I hadn't experienced such discrimination. It impacted me because this monument was built specifically for people like me and my family.

I had a completely different experience a few weeks later when I made a day trip to the Dachau Concentration Camp while visiting Munich. Because I believe in the importance of visiting historical sites, I've now visited several concentration camps on trips to Europe. I hadn't originally planned to visit Munich but added it to my itinerary because I thought it was vital to visit a death camp while I was there.

I arrived and took a tour of the grounds. Toward the end, I stopped by the memorial created in 1968 for the victims of the camp. It consists of three chain links covered with the prisoner patches that each group was forced to wear during the war.

My uncle is an artist and made my dads a beautiful pink triangle to hang on the wall of their home. My sister and I grew up with this emblem in our house, both an image of the torturous past homosexuals endured and a symbol of pride and beauty in who they are today.

I don't remember how long I stood searching for a pink triangle before it finally dawned on me that there wasn't one. I was stunned and my eyes started to fill with tears. I'm sure the people around me thought I was crying for the victims, which I was, but I was crying specifically for those who I couldn't find represented on this so-called memorial. The entire point of visiting this camp was to learn more of the terrible truth about our world's history. And yet, in the place of one of the most horrible atrocities of our recent past, the pain and persecution of some victims of the Holocaust was being ignored.

I couldn't believe that after the incredible feeling of acceptance I had when visiting the Homomonument in Amsterdam I could feel so utterly destroyed at another European destination. Europe has long been considered more progressive and tolerant than the United States, and yet, here I stood at a place that was continuing to disregard Holocaust victims because their deaths were somehow less significant than others.

When I stood in front of the memorial, I didn't know a pink marble triangle stood in the museum. I didn't know the only reason a separate memorial existed was because of decades of protests by local LGBTQ groups. I didn't know the pink marble triangle was first commissioned by these groups in the mid-eighties, only after a request to change the original monument was denied. I didn't know it took another ten years for the memorial to actually be placed in the museum. I didn't know any of this because there was no mention of these facts anywhere around the memorial.[4]

Wanting to educate myself more, I purchased a guidebook for the camp. From this I learned the pink triangle wasn't the only one missing from the monument, so were the black triangle (asocials) and the green triangle (criminals). I also learned this exclusion was a conscious decision by the committee that runs the camp.[5]

Memorials are created not only for those whose lives were lost, but also for future generations, for descendants and those who identify as the same minority group that were persecuted. To have a memorial that ignores three group of victims is like telling every descendent and member of that minority that somehow the deaths of members of their groups didn't matter and that they are easy to forget. In doing so, we continue to persecute these victims and minority groups today. I had gone to the memorial that day with hope, searching for an emblem that wasn't there but left heartbroken, with the message, that once again, society was telling me that my family didn't matter.

꙳

After my time backpacking in Europe and during my last year in college, I decided I wanted to live in Spain and spend a year working, traveling, and becoming fluent in Spanish. I was ecstatic when a Spanish professor told me about a grant for a language and culture assistant position. I applied for the program and before I left New York to backpack through Europe, I received an acceptance letter and placement in Madrid.

When I first moved, I was torn. After years of hiding my family, I had been so happy to move to New York and be honest with everyone. But my time backpacking in Europe left me with conflicted feelings. I admit, I had preconceived notions before my trip. Stereotypically, Europe is supposed to be so much more progressive, whereas the United States is conservative, prudish, and close-minded in comparison. At least that was my perception.

But my three months backpacking brought the realization of how Europe is actually made up of several different countries and cultures, the same way the United States is made up of different states with different policies. And while we often lump them together, this isn't necessarily correct; they have differences. The experiences I had in Amsterdam and Dachau highlighted this point. Some areas are more accepting of homosexuals and others less so, even in Europe. Truthfully, I wasn't sure where Madrid would fall.

My grandmother's family is from Spain, which was part of my desire to go there instead of South America to work on my Spanish. I wanted to see where my ancestors were from. But I also knew from my dad's experience it was a predominantly Catholic country and that this could affect their feelings regarding my family.

I decided to play it by ear in regards to how honest I would be. As I started my job, my gut told me to be careful. There were some staff I was comfortable with and didn't think it would be an issue and others less so. Spaniards are also known for being quite assertive. They're not afraid to share their opinions, which I knew could lead to uncomfortable conversation and work environment if they disagreed with my family structure. As I started work, I stepped back into the shadows. Since I'd spent four years being so open in New York, this was challenging. One day, I slipped up and mentioned Jerry by name instead of saying *my dad*.

"Who's that?" my coworker asked.

"Um …" it had been a long time since I'd had to lie about his presence in my life. "He's my uncle, he lives in town and he's not married so he spends a lot of time with our family." I pulled the high school lie from my back pocket. Spain is a very family-oriented country, so it wasn't strange to them to have my uncle present at all of our family holidays and events.

During my time in Spain, I met some great American girls who I became close to. I met them during training. We were all there for the same program. Maria was looking for an apartment and there was another room available where I was renting. I told her about it and after checking it out, she moved in. We were only at that apartment for about a month. Shortly after moving in, we started experiencing issues with our roommate who owned the place.

One day, he was unhappy about something and he came into my room when I was on the phone with my mom. He started screaming at me in Spanish. My mother instantly became concerned, "Natalie, are you sure you're safe there? If you don't feel safe, leave. I don't care about the deposit or what it costs for a hotel. Your dad and I will pay for it if need be."

I assured her that I was fine and that he wasn't violent even though he yelled a lot. The next day when Maria and I left for work, I told her, "I've been thinking about finding a new apartment, but I didn't want to leave you there with him."

"I've been thinking the same thing!" she stated. "Let's start looking for other places so we can still live together."

We were fortunate to find a place quickly, although it had just been renovated and didn't have any furniture yet. We had to pay the deposit immediately to hold the apartment even though we couldn't move in for a few weeks.

I called my dad and, for the first time in my life, asked him for money. It was one of the hardest things I've ever done, and I felt terrible. I generally manage money very well, but this move meant we had to pay a second deposit on an apartment. I hadn't planned for this extra expense, and since we'd only been there a few weeks I hadn't received a paycheck yet.

My dad knew about my living situation. One thing about having parents who stayed friends after their divorce is that they talked on a regular basis. I was sure my mom had told him about the incident that happened when we were on the phone.

I apologized profusely and promised I would pay him back as soon as I received my first check but asked that he deposit $350 into my account so I could secure the apartment. My dad agreed to loan me the money and added, "Natalie, I know this is difficult for you and I'm very proud of you for coming to me and asking for a loan when you need it. You're all the way across the world, and I want to have peace of mind that you're in a good living situation. Besides, this is a good learning lesson for you: sometimes being an adult means knowing when to ask for help."

Because our roommate had become increasingly difficult to live with, we wanted to move out at the end of the month. Our new landlord wanted to push back the move-in date so that he could get the apartment completely furnished. We explained our bad living situation and that we had to move as soon as possible. We told him we didn't care if it took him a couple of weeks after we moved in to get the rest of the furniture. We would just sleep on the floor for a bit. He seemed a little concerned by our response and agreed to let us move in a few days.

At the end of the month, Maria and I waited for our roommate to leave and then packed up our stuff. We left our keys on the counter with a sticky note stating, "We moved today." He'd already threatened that if we ever moved out he would keep our deposits, so we made the decision to forfeit the money and avoid a potentially sketchy situation. We were pleasantly surprised when we arrived at our new place and found it completely furnished and ready.

Maria was a great roommate, and I felt incredibly comfortable with her. As we met others and formed a regular group of friends, I knew I could be honest with them and told them about my family. I've found many Americans who travel internationally tend to be more liberal in their views and more accepting of people's differences. It would be very difficult for those who are close-minded to be successful in their work and daily lives if they weren't accepting of the culture in which they were living.

Living overseas for the first time, I finally understood people's mentality of wanting to spend time with others like them. It's funny, for those who didn't grow up as a minority, they don't realize how strange and trying it can be to always be surrounded by people that are unlike them in some way. It takes a lot of energy to try to be accepted in a culture that's not your own.

In Spain, I did have friends from other countries, both Spaniards and some from other English-speaking countries, but there was a certain comfort that came from spending time with people whom I had more in common with. With my American friends, we shared a language where one of us wasn't making an intentional effort to speak properly or use vocabulary that the other person would understand. They grasped the need to make occasional trips to the American store for ingredients for Thanksgiving, or the desire to periodically watch an American movie that hadn't been dubbed over in Spanish. We found a commonality in our appetite for American establishments that served blended alcoholic beverages, something that wasn't typical in most Spanish bars. There's something refreshing about hanging out from time to time with people who know your culture and language, especially when in another country.

Even after backpacking through Europe, I still experienced some culture shock in Spain. I found that people in some parts of Europe have a different attitude about helping friends, especially with moving. After Maria and I moved to our new apartment we decided to buy a sofa bed as we both expected to have more friends and family visit throughout the year. We found one used but the seller lived outside the metro zone. We couldn't find any teachers with a car who were willing to help, so we decided to take public transit to pick it up. We asked our English and Irish friends if they would help and they all declined. "It's your sofa," they said.

Maria, three of our friends, and I went down to pick it up. When we got to the house, we called a cab and put all of the cushions in the trunk and backseat, and I rode back to the apartment with them. The rest of our group carried the frame back to the metro zone. We weren't allowed to take it on the bus, but pretty much anything can be taken on the metro, so once they got to that zone they could use public transit to get back.

Some of our non-American friends thought we were crazy to go through all that work to get a sofa bed, and they didn't understand why our friends helped. We tried to explain it's just what Americans do; we always help our friends move. Plus, as Maria and my friends pointed out, they would all benefit from the sofa bed. Maria and I lived in the center of town, and now they could all crash there after a night out instead of having to cram into the night buses to get back to their place. Regardless, I loved that we now had a story of five American girls with a *can do* attitude schlepping a sofa bed across Madrid.

҈

My family and I continued our weekly calls, and my mom continued to send a care package every month. My dad upgraded and instead of handwriting letters every week, he started sending daily emails. He would include the whole family so we could simply hit *reply all* and keep us up on everyone's lives.

Unlike when I was living in New York, I didn't fly home for the holidays. It was too expensive, and I wanted to travel as much as I could while in Europe. I spent every long weekend and school vacation seeing a new place. I was able to visit Morocco, Portugal, Poland, and travel all around Spain.

It turned out it was a good thing we'd gone through all of that work to get the sofa bed, because we had quite a few visitors that year, including my mom. Since I didn't go home for Christmas my mom decided to make a trip out to Madrid in the spring.

She showed up exhausted after several airport delays. I, being a big city cheapskate, insisted we take the subway back to my apartment. As we hauled her bag up and down three different sets of escalators due to the several metro transfers, she looked at me and tiredly pleaded, "Next time, please just let me pay for a taxi, okay?"

When we got to my neighborhood, she was slightly horrified as we turned down my street. I'd tried to warn her beforehand that it was a safe area, but that it was also one of the most popular streets in the city for prostitutes.

"Natalie, you didn't tell me there were that many women on your street!" she declared. "I can't believe this is where you're living!"

Her fears calmed as we entered the apartment. "This is really nice," she told me as she looked around. "You have granite countertops? I don't even have granite in my house," she said with a hint of jealously.

We got her settled in the living room, and I showed her how to pull out the bed. She decided to take a little nap before we went to dinner. We spent a week together, seeing all the sites in Madrid and traveling to Cordoba. It was Easter week, so she got to enjoy the processionals after getting over her shock about their outfits. Spaniards wore white cloaks with head coverings, which can be startling for Americans if they don't know what to expect. I forgot to give my mom a heads up, and she looked out the hotel window in Cordoba to see hundreds of people dressed eerily similar to the KKK marching down the street.

We had a great mother and daughter time. My mom particularly enjoyed the food, although commented she was eating nonstop. After being in town for a few days I inquired where she wanted to go for tapas and she asked, "Is it time to eat again already?"

By the end of the trip, I was sad to see her go. My mom and I are pretty similar, so sometimes we can butt heads. However, we'd made it the whole trip without any disagreements. It was also nice to get the chance to travel with my mom and share such an important part of my life.

❧

Since I wasn't honest about my family with many people outside my close group of friends, I didn't often have the opportunity to challenge people's judgment about the gay community. But one weekend, I'd taken a trip with a friend to the Basque country in northern Spain. Our first night in the hostel we were sitting with a group chatting when I overheard a group of Irish guys making fun of a gay couple they'd seen that day. One of them noticed me looking at them and asked, "Don't you think that's crazy?"

"To be honest, I don't really understand your fascination. As long as everyone involved are consenting adults, I don't really care what people do in their bedroom."

The smile disappeared from his face, and he stood there for a moment, silent. Finally, he responded, "Well, how the hell can you argue with that?"

Meanwhile, I was enjoying the Culture and Language Assistant program I participated in that year. While I liked being in the classroom, I didn't really feel a call to be a teacher. But my time in Spain did teach me a couple things about myself.

First of all, I loved travelling and wanted to live overseas again. When I moved to Spain, my plan was to take one year off from school to travel and become fluent in Spanish and then return to New York to apply for a graduate program in anthropology so I could continue my fieldwork on polyamory and publish academically. But as I spent a year living, working, and traveling in Europe, I decided I didn't want to sit in a classroom to learn about the world. I'd rather learn from personal experience.

Second, I wanted to return home short term and spend time with my family. A couple of months before the school year ended, my uncle died of cancer. I had called my aunt to check in with her and the family when suddenly she cried, "Oh my God!" and slammed down the phone. She realized he was taking his last breaths and hung up to run to his bedside. After being away from my family for five years, his death really affected me because I realized the distance I'd put between myself and Idaho also separated me from my family and made it difficult to be there when they needed me.

Finally, I really wanted to get into volunteer work again. I hadn't done much in college or while in Europe and being in the classroom made me realize I missed helping people. I'd done some research on different programs and there was one that would allow me to do all the above. I decided to return to Idaho briefly while I applied for the Peace Corps.

Forever Trapped

I'm lying in my bed
Looking at the book
I try to get away
But once again I'm hooked

For time again
I take the flight
The tormenting kind
I cannot fight

My thoughts take me to the Holocaust
With people all around
I try to hide
But I get knocked down

I run to my surroundings
But there lies only walls
I have nowhere to escape
Except the holes to which I fall

Farther and farther
In this terrible place
Nowhere to go
No familiar face

I dream of freedom
Yet get whipped on the back
I'm forced to work
Until my legs crack

When the guards come
To take me away
To do worse things
I want to stay

Is it better to be
Here or gone?
I lie to myself
Creating a con

Of a peaceful life
Where there is no hate
I'm still stuck
Dying is my fate

Do the Nazis feel?
Do they want us to die?
I know they do
I see it in their eye

I feel their hate
See their fear
They strike us down
By words we hear

People we met yesterday
They'll never be seen again
They're taken to gas chambers
By the world's worst men

Camps are finally liberated
But my pride is forever trapped
My sanity has disappeared
My feelings; they are capped

I'm struck back to reality
Forced to rest my head
But there is sorrow in my heart
I know why my ancestors are dead

7 Peace Corps

When I left Madrid in 2007, I returned to Idaho for several months. I was excited to see my family because it'd been a long time since I'd spent a significant amount of time with them. Since the goal was to be there only a while as I applied for the Peace Corps, it didn't seem practical to sign a lease for an apartment and buy furniture, so my mom agreed to let me live with her. She still charged me rent, although it was pretty cheap.

I was apprehensive about my return. In New York I was open and unapologetic about my family. While I was more guarded in Spain, all of my closest friends had known about and accepted my family. Moving back to Idaho meant giving all of that up. I'd been gone for five years and hadn't kept in touch with many people from high school. I would need to find a new job and make new friends. Once again, I would need to be cautious who I told about my family.

My first step when I got back was to start looking for jobs. I applied for everything I was qualified for. I didn't worry too much about finding a job I loved since I wouldn't be there for long. I landed a few interviews within a couple weeks of returning home. After some dud ones, I knew wouldn't lead to anything, I had a successful interview and got an offer at an OBGYN's office. It was my first job in health care.

The entry-level administrative job allowed me to see all the newborn babies when patients would come in for their six-week postpartum appointments. While I enjoyed the work, I also struggled with some of my new coworkers.

Nancy, one of the women I worked with, was very religious. While she had a good heart and really cared about people, she also spent most of her days talking about religion and God. It was a small clinic, so it was impossible to escape these conversations. Sometimes she would want to discuss her religion with me, other times it was with patients or staff members. She wasn't trying to convert me, but her having the ability to talk about her faith so freely bothered me, especially since I couldn't be open about my family.

While I did share with a couple of coworkers, I couldn't tell most of them about my upbringing. I spent Monday mornings lying about what I'd done over the weekend or leaving Jerry out of my stories. I felt like I had taken ten steps backward. I realized how hard it was, once I had a taste of freedom, to go back to the way things were. In return this made me quite angry, and I found myself eager to leave the state again.

After a few months in my new job, I submitted my Peace Corps application. The process went quickly. I interviewed shortly after submitting the paperwork. During my interview, I stressed my desire to participate in an HIV/AIDS program in Africa. They asked me about working in education since I'd done the Language and Cultural Assistant program in Spain, but I really wanted to focus on health. Since I didn't have much experience, they suggested I start doing volunteer work. After my interview, I reached out to Allies Linked for the Prevention of HIV and AIDS (ALPHA). I did my training and immediately started volunteering in their office. I answered calls and scheduled testing appointments. I also read all the information available and would talk with the staff whenever I could. Soon thereafter I started participating in the Condom Raids in downtown Boise where they would distribute free condoms on Friday and Saturday nights.

I completed the rest of my paperwork so I could get my dental and medical clearance. Everything went fairly smoothly, but when they called to tell me that I'd gotten my dental and medical approval, they also informed me the health program I had originally been nominated for was already filled. I was given the option of waiting another year for the next health program or doing an education program in Madagascar. Based on my experience working at the bilingual school in Madrid, they encouraged me to go into education. I considered my options; knowing that I wasn't very happy in my current position and didn't want to spend another year in Idaho swayed me to do the education program.

The next six months were a struggle because I was anxious to leave. I was ready to travel and see more of the world and really wanted to help people. In retrospect, while my time in Idaho had me feeling a bit like a caged animal, it was good prep prior to Peace Corps service.

When it came time to leave for Madagascar, I was stressed. I had received a packing list from the volunteers currently serving in the country. While it was helpful, there was a lot of information. To make it more challenging, the climate varies greatly depending on what part of the country being lived in. We wouldn't get our site selections until we arrived and started our training.

The day before I left, I was sitting in my room on the floor with my backpack surrounded by everything I needed. I had my list but was almost in tears as I was trying to figure out how I was going to get everything in my bag and make sure I wasn't missing anything. Unbeknownst to me, my sister had talked to her boss to see if she could get off early. Suddenly, she was standing in the doorway of my room. "Need some help?"

"I have everything I'm supposed to but I have so many piles and I'm trying to go through my list and make sure it's all here and get it organized and put in my bag. I'm worried that I might be missing some things, but they should be here somewhere," I started rattling without taking a single breath.

"Give me the list, Natalie," she gently commanded. "We'll go through it item by item and make sure you have everything."

She sat there with me for at least an hour, reading items off and then crossing things off as I packed them. Occasionally, I would remember something I needed that I hadn't written down, and she would add it to the list and then grab it for me. It reminded me of my conversation with her at the hostel in New York. For some reason, she always seems to be there for me when I'm really stressed and when I need somebody to help me get through the day. I often think of her as my anchor, guiding me through challenges, encouraging me, and reminding me that I can do the task at hand.

Because of her help, I got done early. I had a few hours to spare and, instead of sitting in the house, I wanted to do something fun to relax. Katie suggested we see a movie. There weren't many that aligned with the time at hand, especially since we only had a few hours before a family goodbye dinner. But *Kung Fu Panda* was playing, and we thought an animated film would be perfect: fun and silly was exactly what we were looking for. It was a perfect way to end our afternoon and make a final sister memory before I left the country for two years. It's still one of our favorite memories from that time, and every time we think of it, it makes us both smile.

It was a long trek to get to Madagascar. I first had a flight from Idaho to New York. Due to many technical issues and delays, it took over twenty hours. I finally arrived at the hotel after midnight, checked in, got my keycard, and went up to my room. When I got to the door, I couldn't open it. Thinking that maybe they had given me the wrong room number and not wanting to wake anyone up if that was the case, I went back down to the front desk to double check. They had indeed given me the correct room, but my roommate, Kelly, had locked the deadbolt, thinking I wasn't coming until the next day. They called the room and woke her up and asked that she unlock the door for me. I was so exhausted I threw my bag down on the floor and lay on the bed still dressed in my clothes. Kelly and I were both so excited about our Peace Corps service and being headed to Africa that we ended up staying up and talking for hours.

The next day we started orientation. The Peace Corps likes to do an in-service while volunteers are still in the United States to make sure everyone understands what they're getting themselves into before they fly them to their host country. There are some people who early terminate (ET) during this time, but everyone in my stage ended up on the plane two days later.

We were all excited and a little nervous. While most people were concerned about the living arrangements, safety, or culture shock, I wasn't overly worried. By this point, I'd studied in Mexico and China, backpacked through Europe by myself, and lived in Spain. I was well traveled, bilingual, and had a background in anthropology. I didn't expect it to be too hard to adjust. However, I was nervous because I was acutely aware I was headed into a new environment where I would once again have to gauge the culture to determine how to handle talking about my family structure and religion.

The Peace Corps accepted people in the LGBTQ community far before I became a volunteer. However, they cautioned volunteers to think carefully about where they were serving and the implications if the community wasn't accepting of homosexuality. Most gay volunteers choose to hide their sexual orientation in their host communities. While the organization has long accepted LGBTQ individuals, they still hadn't changed their policy to accept gay couples. The first same-sex couple wouldn't serve until 2013, and positions are limited as they can't serve in countries where homosexuality is criminalized.[1] We made our way to Antananarivo, the capital of Madagascar. Once we touched down at the airport, we still had a long drive to Alarobia to meet our host families and begin our three-month training in education. Teaching in Madagascar was going to be quite different from my experience in Spain. In addition to educational training, we would study their culture, hear about health risks, and learn the Malagasy language.

Upon arrival, we were taken to the training site and assigned our host families. My first night in Madagascar I went home with my family. I only knew a few words of Malagasy. When my host mom took me to my room, she showed me a blue bucket with a lid on it. She put it on the floor, took the lid off, and then squatted over it to show me this was what I was supposed to use if I had to go to the bathroom in the middle of the night. All I could think was that I wished I had a companion named Toto with me to share I definitely was not in Kansas anymore.

The next morning after a silent breakfast, I headed back to the Peace Corps building to start our training. I had three months to learn how to teach in a country where the class sizes could range from sixty to a hundred students, where the schools often didn't have electricity, and where classrooms sometimes didn't have enough desks for all the students. I also needed to learn how to adjust to living in a country where women have fewer rights and how to endure living in a country where religion is vital to their culture.

Peace Corps staff educated trainees on their policies, including how to handle different situations. "If you as a volunteer become unable to complete your service, regardless of the reason or even whether it's your fault, we could ask you to leave the Peace Corps."

We all sat in silence for a moment. Finally, a girl raised her hand, "Can you give us an example of when something like that might happen? Especially the *not our fault* part?"

"Sure. A couple of years ago we had a young woman who was suspected of having an affair with a married man in her town. While she denied the allegations, it ultimately didn't matter. The rumors had spread across town and made it impossible for her to be successful in her role. In the end, we had to send her home."

I understood the reason behind this policy; our government spent a lot of money to send volunteers to serve in countries with the expectation they would be providing necessary aid. If that work couldn't be done, it was a waste of their time and resources. It could also hurt the relationship between the Peace Corps and the host country and create obstacles for future volunteers.

With that said, this example made me very afraid. I knew for sure I wouldn't be able to be honest about my family, but the even bigger problem would be my lack of religion.

In Madagascar, asking someone's religion is like asking about someone's work in the United States. When meeting someone for the first time, the conversation goes as follows: "Hi, I'm Lova, what's your name?"

"Natalie, it's nice to meet you."

"You too. What religion are you?"

"Um…"

Yes, I could skirt the issue somewhat by educating people that Americans don't really share their religious beliefs after just meeting someone. But it quickly became obvious to everyone in my small town that I didn't go to *any* of the local churches. As the only foreigner in town, my actions were often a topic for discussion.

Knowing my lack of religion would be difficult for the Malagasy people to understand and also knowing my reasons for not being religious would be impossible to explain, I fell back on an ageless crutch: I lied.

Like all lies, it's better to base them somewhat in truth because they're easier to remember down the road. When asked about not going to church, I told them my family bounced around a bit between churches, so I wasn't partial to one over another. They would always follow up by asking if I was a Christian to which I answered yes.

To this day, I wonder about some of my relationships from that time. I believe there are levels of friendship. I'm genuinely curious how my service would have been affected if I had been honest with the people in my town. And while I keep in contact with some Malagasy friends today, I still haven't told them the truth. Part of me would like to, but part of me is still unsure of whether I want to know if they would still be my friend if they knew the real me.

That's the interesting thing about living on the outskirts of societal norms. Over the years, I've learned quickly who my true friends were. And for those I wasn't sure of, those who I didn't trust entirely, I just lied to them about aspects of my life. I always questioned if they would still like me if I was completely honest.

Having a gay family, which is part of my identity, helped shape who I am. I can't remove that part of me or have real relationships with people if they don't know or understand that. Yes, I have acquaintances who I haven't told, but our relationships can only go so deep, because there's always part of me and my perception of the world that they will never truly understand.

When it came to my host family, I considered myself lucky because my host mom was a Malagasy teacher. Every night I would do my homework, and she would review it. She would also teach me new words and quiz me on vocabulary. I remember thinking how fortunate I was to have a host family who cared about making sure I learned as much of the language as I could while living with them. I was also grateful my host mom had the skills to teach me more about their language and grammar. About six weeks into our training we received the location of our site placement. I was not surprised that my site, Antanifotsy, was located only a couple of hours from the capital and about an hour from another major city. I have asthma and, while it's well-controlled and didn't prevent me from being accepted into the Peace Corps, I figured they would probably put me in close proximity to a major city just in case I had any issues.

Again, I was very fortunate. My town believed education was important. I taught junior high, high school, and adults. Many of my junior high students would walk five or more miles each way to attend my class. There were even fewer high schools, so most of the students lived in town Monday through Friday and only returned home on weekends.

I've never been so aware of my privilege as I was when living in Madagascar. Living in a community where eighty percent of the population lives in poverty and many families live on less than a dollar a day was eye opening. I'd dealt with some emotional struggles growing up, but I always had a roof over my head and food on my plate. I never lacked anything I truly needed. I could always find a job when I wanted work, even if it wasn't always a job I enjoyed. I had a good education from an amazing school. I had the ability to move across the country and to travel the world. I had no idea what it was to struggle just to survive.

Once I saw what my students went through every day just to get an education, I was inspired. They were some of the most motivated people I'd ever encountered, and teaching them became an absolute joy. I fell in love with my job and my service, but unfortunately, my time in the Peace Corps was cut short. After a while at our sites, there was a political coup. I ended up being in the capital at the time. I had a chronic ear infection that had lasted two and a half months. I'd taken multiple antibiotics, but they weren't working. Finally, the Peace Corps doctors decided I needed to see a specialist so they insisted I go to the capital. I thought I was going to be there overnight. However, the morning after my appointment I was packing my bag to return to the site when I overhead voices downstairs.

"Did you hear about the unrest?"

"I've heard some people say that they're not sure if it's safe to go to the station."

"My friends in town are telling me to stay put."

I walked downstairs to join the conversation. "What's going on?" I asked.

"There are rumors that there are riots in the city center. I've heard they're trying to overthrow the president."

"Seriously?" I asked. "What do we do? I'm getting ready to head to the station to go back to my site. Is that safe?"

"Honestly, I don't know. We've called the Peace Corps. I think we should stay put until we hear back from them. You can always take a later ride if it turns out the rumors aren't true but I think it's better to play it safe."

It didn't take long for the Peace Corps to get back to us and confirm the rumors were true. We were safe at Peace Corps Meva (the name of our transit house), so we were temporarily placed on lockdown while they determined the severity of the situation and next steps. The seven of us in the capital were kept at the Meva for a week and only allowed to leave occasionally to go to the main Peace Corps office to help with the consolidation plans for the other volunteers. Such plans are always in place in the event unrest occurs and the country becomes unsafe. Unfortunately, in this situation, many of the planned consolidation points were areas they were still experiencing riots, which meant that they needed to develop a plan B.

There were approximately 140 volunteers in Madagascar at the time and, while cell phone service had expanded quite a bit, not everybody had reception. Communicating with all the volunteers about where they were going to move and when they were going to be picked up was quite a process. The conference room had a big map with a pin for every volunteer and notes about who had been contacted, who was going where, and what Peace Corps drivers needed to go to what locations to pick up volunteers. Finally, after a week everyone was consolidated and the riots had calmed.

Those of us at the Meva were taken to the training camp in Mantasoa. There were about eighty volunteers housed there while the other sixty were still at other consolidation points around the country. Things calmed down drastically toward the end of the week, but staff was still not sure the coup was over. The former president had been ousted, and there were still occasional spontaneous disruptions across the country. For another three weeks, we stayed at the training camp getting updates twice a day while they tried to determine whether we would stay or if the Peace Corps should pull out of the country.

Throughout the month I was offsite, I texted daily with my family to pass along the updates we'd been given from the staff. Unfortunately, due to bad cell phone service in the area we weren't able to talk on the phone. My parents have always been very supportive of my travels, but I know my time in Madagascar was particularly challenging for them. During the coup, they didn't have much access to news because the country isn't often covered in American news. Most of the reports available were through French outlets. My family would then have to use online translation, which tends to be inaccurate, to get the information.

After three weeks at the training camp, the Peace Corps decided it was safe to stay in the country and sent all of us back to our sites. I tried to settle in, but after being so unprepared when the first consolidation happened, I organized what few possessions I had and created piles for what I would take and what I would leave if things were to flare up again.

My dads had been planning a trip to Madagascar when the coup occurred. They were in the process of researching places to visit and preparing to buy plane tickets.

"I'm worried that they won't like it here," I'd told my sister a short time before. "Dad especially isn't very outdoorsy and they're accustomed to a certain lifestyle. There are some great cities here that would be fun to visit but they also lack real Malagasy culture because they're largely populated by expats."

"Well, they want to see where you live too. You said you have some sort of a 'hotel,' right?"

"Haha, yeah. The owner of the one small store rents out a couple rooms above it. I haven't seen them."

"Check it out. They could spend a day or two in your town, meet your friends, and get a sense of the culture. Then you could spend the rest of the time doing things more their style. Honestly, Natalie, they've heard your stories; they have a sense of what it's like where you live. I don't think they expect anything fancy. They just really want to see you."

The coup put their plans on hold. A month after returning to my site, the military decided to get involved in the debate about who was running the country. Military members were divided about which side they supported and, at that point, everyone was afraid things could escalate again. It's not good when the people with guns don't agree. All of the international aid organizations pulled out of the country, including the Peace Corps. I received a call on a Wednesday night from our security office telling me to take the first ride out the next morning and not to tell anyone I wouldn't be back.

As the Peace Corps volunteers regrouped, many were talking about how difficult it was to say goodbye to people they would never see again without telling them it was indeed a final goodbye. In my case this was challenging too, but I had already been dishonest with them for months about my family and religion. This was just one more lie.

It took four days for the Peace Corps to evacuate all of the volunteers. We were flown to South Africa. Johannesburg wasn't known for being safe at the time and was off-limits to volunteers. We were taken to a hotel where we were again not allowed to leave the campus. For the first time in a long time, I had an actual phone conversation with my family.

I told them when I would be coming home but that I then planned to transfer to South America to finish my service. This news was challenging for my dad. After all of the ups and downs and emotional turmoil my whole family had gone through for the past two months, the notion I wanted to continue volunteering overseas where something like this could occur again did not give him any peace of mind. Fortunately, my dad has always been supportive, and while he may not have thought it was the best idea, he did respect my choice.

When I returned to United States in 2009, I found the situation had changed dramatically. The economy had crashed while I was overseas, and the number of applications the Peace Corps received increased astronomically. In addition, we returned at the end of March, so most of the summer programs were already full. Most of us were told we would have to wait another year to be placed. Of course, after volunteering for almost a year and giving up my job, car, apartment, and steady paycheck to do so, there was absolutely no way I could afford to live for a year not knowing if I would be accepted back into the Peace Corps.

As it was, it took them three months to close out our bank accounts, and I was so grateful to have a family to lean on. My mom allowed me to live with her, this time without paying rent, because otherwise I would have been homeless. My family understood I was at a crossroads. My mom patiently told me to take some time to figure out where exactly I wanted to go from there.

I started looking at options and decided I still wanted to volunteer. If I couldn't do so through the Peace Corps, then I was going to start looking at AmeriCorps programs where I could continue teaching English as a Second Language.

Fallen

We are the falling leaves
The Fallen
Every time we take a step
    We fall
Every time we start to love
    We fall
How is it we find the strength to keep trying?
Maybe it's the hope of rejuvenation
When spring comes
We are the blossoming trees
Full of life
Of happiness
We are once again alive
Wishing that we could stay that way
But knowing that soon enough
We will once again fall

8 AmeriCorps

I had fallen in love with teaching while in Madagascar. While I appreciated all my students, my favorite class was the one I taught at the Community English Center, which was geared toward adults. After being evacuated, I still wanted to give back but knew I didn't want to stay in Idaho and wasn't ready to put down roots. I wanted to live in a large city again, be around diverse groups of people and enjoy good weather, so I applied through AmeriCorps to different education programs in Los Angeles.

After submitting applications, I got call from Gina, a former high school teacher and friend. She worked with Partners of the Americas in Boise. They were planning a trip to Ecuador in a couple of months. They were supposed to conduct a workshop on how to teach English as a second language (ESL), but one of the teachers had backed out at the last minute. She knew I had just returned early from my Peace Corps service and wanted to know if I was interested in going to South America.

I jumped at the opportunity. I was still waiting to hear about the AmeriCorps programs I'd applied for, so I wasn't really doing anything at the time. I quickly submitted the required paperwork so the organization could approve the change in staff. I also had to prepare topics and handouts for two weeks' worth of lectures. The workshop was being held at the Catholic University in Cuenca. Teachers and professors from the entire region would be attending, so I wanted to be organized. Because of the location, I was also reminded of how strongly the Catholic religion opposed homosexuality. Since I was only going to be there for a few weeks, I decided it would be easier if I didn't mention my dads to anyone.

Only three months after I returned from my Peace Corps service, I was on a plane again. Gina had been to Ecuador before, so we went down a couple of weeks early to spend time with her friends in Quito and Riobamba before the workshop started. I had a fantastic time and met many amazing people. The trip was great for my Spanish too, as I hadn't used those language skills for nearly a year. In Madagascar, I had learned Malagasy and hadn't used Spanish at all. While I've spoken Spanish for many years, putting it on the backburner for so long meant I needed some time to regain my fluid speaking skills.

The difficult part about being in Ecuador was that right before I left I received a couple of calls for the AmeriCorps programs to which I'd applied. They only had a few weeks to conduct their interviews, which meant I would have to do them long distance. Looking back, I think being overseas worked in my favor. I was applying for ESL teaching jobs after all, and I was in Ecuador conducting an ESL workshop.

I was fortunate to get accepted into the AmeriCorps program that was my top choice, so shortly after I returned from Ecuador, I packed up my car and moved to Los Angeles in August 2009. My mom went with me to help me get settled and find an apartment. I appreciated her willingness to help, although we joked afterwards it didn't do much good to have her there. We found a place with two women who told us they were college students. The day after my mom left, I was sitting in my bedroom when I heard a commotion. One of my roommates knocked on my door. "What's going on?" I asked as I opened the door.

"Well, Magda has a client here and he's a little upset," she said.

"A client?"

"Yes, she likes to make a little extra money by advertising herself on Craigslist."

My roommates were actually prostitutes who brought their johns home. The commotion was because Magda was a transgendered woman, and her client didn't understand what the T/S stood for online. He paid and then got upset when he saw her downstairs equipment. She refused to give his money back, which made matters worse.

I called my sister that afternoon and told her what had happened. Once she stopped laughing in disbelief she said, "Natalie, you have to move."

"I know, but I just moved in and it's so much work to pack everything up again. Plus, I start my orientation tomorrow. I don't have time to look at apartments this week."

"You have to move. I get that it's frustrating and you have a lot going on, but it's not safe if they're bringing the guys home, especially if sometimes they don't understand that they're hiring a transgender prostitute and get angry. He could get violent or come back later looking for his money."

"I know, I know … it's just such a pain."

My mom felt horrible when I told her. She felt partially responsible for not figuring out that it was an unsavory living situation, even though I assured her there was no way to know that they were prostitutes. They had flat out lied about their occupations.

The funny part is that I'm pretty accepting and my boundaries are pretty far out there. I didn't care that Magda was transgendered and suspected so when I met her. Growing up in a gay family, such things weren't a defining factor in who I live with. I also didn't care she was a prostitute. I've never understood why people can have sex with whoever they want for free, but somehow it's illegal when people do it for money. What bothered me about the situation was that they brought their clients back to the place I was living.

I didn't have a computer at the time or a smartphone because I'd just moved back to the United States and had used the last of my Peace Corps money to move to Los Angeles. I was borrowing an old-school cell from my sister. My mom ended up looking at places online and setting up appointments for me to look at apartments, and then texting me the details.

A couple of days later, she sent me the details for an amazing place. I went to look and it had a huge master bedroom, walk-in closet, and private bathroom. I couldn't believe it was so cheap. When I asked the couple renting it out, they told me the house had belonged to their parents. They wanted to sell it, but when the economy crashed they couldn't get much for it, so they'd decided to rent it out. Since then, their niece had decided to move to the United States from Vietnam for college. She had one of the rooms, and they wanted to rent the others to college students so everyone would be in the same age bracket. They knew most college kids couldn't afford expensive places so they kept the rent cheap.

Even though I wasn't in college, I was a young woman, teacher, and AmeriCorps volunteer, so they accepted my application. I was so excited to move into the new apartment. I went home that night and found my roommate sitting on the couch crying, "What's wrong?" I asked as I walked through the door.

"Well, Magda went to Las Vegas for a few days. She accidently solicited an undercover cop so they arrested her. The search found drugs and since she already had an immigration hold, they're deporting her back to El Salvador," she sniffled. "On the bright side, this takes care of the prostitution thing so you'll be more comfortable living here now."

The fact that my druggie, prostitute roommate was about to be deported didn't change the situation.

That weekend, I moved into my new place. I was so grateful the rest of the AmeriCorps volunteers helped me move. When I told them about my living situation they couldn't believe it. Even though they'd only known me for a week, they all offered assistance.

The following week, I started work at the nonprofit where I had been placed for my AmeriCorps service. They were looking to start a new family literacy program and brought me onboard because of my time in Spain and my Peace Corps experience. They also hired my counterpart, Amanda, who had teaching experience in China. They were hoping between the two of us we would have the skills to build a new program.

It was a lot of work; neither of us were familiar with the neighborhood, so first we had to figure out what resources existed and assess the community's needs and wants. Through our research, we determined a family literacy program wouldn't work. Most of the parents were literate in Spanish while most of their children were literate in English. Such a program when there wasn't a common language was next to impossible.

But we did find that many of the parents wanted to improve their English-speaking skills. They were disappointed they couldn't help their kids with homework, couldn't talk to their kids' teachers if there was an issue at school, or they didn't qualify for a work promotion because they lacked fluency in English. With this information, Amanda and I went back to our supervisor and pitched the idea of creating an adult ESL program. Our nonprofit was supportive so Amanda and I went to work.

We networked in the community, established how our program would run, created assessments, developed marketing materials, advertised, and wrote curriculum for five different class levels over two years. Our first year, nine students completed our pilot program and by the end of the year we had ninety on our waiting list for the fall term.

We encountered many cultural issues and realized one of the gaps in our marketing when someone called us from another organization in town asking about whether we required proof of citizenship for students to enroll. This wasn't something we had thought of nor was it something we required. It made us realize that we hadn't communicated this to the community and how it was affecting whether people were comfortable reaching out for additional information. Some of the immigrants were not there legally and were too terrified to even call to see if this was a specification.

While my time in Ecuador helped, my Spanish-speaking skills were still quite rusty, and I was grateful to have the opportunity to speak with my students. Amanda only spoke basic Spanish, so I was responsible for all the phone calls and interviews and marketing in the Spanish-speaking community. I really enjoyed the work; it was fantastic for me to work in a community organization and to be able to go out and work with groups of different people. It also helped to keep my Spanish-speaking skills fluid.

While my time in AmeriCorps gave me valuable skills such as learning how to build a new program from the ground up, marketing, community assessment, writing curriculum, program development, and project management, it was also one of my most uncomfortable times away from home.

I knew my placement would be personally challenging my first Friday there. Carrie, the founder, ordered lunch for everyone, which was a nice gesture. But when everyone gathered at the table, we were told to bow our heads for prayer. I sat in stunned silence at the request, especially since it wasn't a religious organization. While I'm a strong advocate of volunteer work and know that numerous religious organizations provide good services, I tend to avoid them. Because I'm not religious, I'm simply not comfortable working for those types of organizations.

I found prayer was a routine activity at group meals. Since it was a small organization and I was uncomfortable announcing my lack of religion to my new co-workers, I stopped attending the lunches. After a few weeks, my supervisor, Renee, asked me about it.

"I'm not comfortable with the expectation of group prayer at these lunches. This isn't a religious organization and while I don't mind if others want to pray by themselves, I find the assumption that everyone is Christian and wanting to pray at work a little offensive and unwelcoming. It also puts me in an awkward situation to then discuss religion at work, which I personally don't feel is appropriate."

Renee replied, "I really appreciate you being honest with me. I will talk to Carrie. You're right, this isn't a religious organization. As a little background, those of us that started this non-profit did so after meeting at church. I think we've adopted some practices based on our beginnings. But we have grown and expanded quite a bit in the past few years and we should make sure we're being respectful of all of our staff."

That should've been my first clue that maybe this wasn't an environment that would be accepting of my family, but Renee had been so responsive to my concerns about religion in the workplace that I didn't think too much of it. I had decorated my workspace and, for the first time in my life, I'd put a family photo on my desk.

Most straight people never even think about putting out pictures. You walk by desks in almost any office in the United States and see people have pictures of their kids, their spouse, their parents, and their pets. For a person with a gay family, taking a family photo to work can be a great cause of anxiety. Will people ask about it? How much detail should be provided? Will others judge? What if a coworker finds it offensive or asks that the photo be taken down? When I moved to Los Angeles I thought that I was finally in an environment where I could decorate my desk as I wanted.

I took a photo of the five of us from our Christmas trip in Mexico. It's one of my favorite pictures because we all have big smiles on our faces and you can tell how genuinely happy we are. It didn't take long for coworkers to ask about it; everyone seemed to genuinely want to get to know Amanda and me. I always told them it was my family: my two dads, mom, and sister. I learned quickly not everyone in the office was okay with my family situation. While most people just stopped asking about them, especially when I went home over the holidays, there was one colleague who took the opportunity to give me a thirty-minute lecture about how being gay is a sin.

I was cornered at my desk with no escape from the verbal attack. When she finally stopped talking, she left and I sat at my desk close to tears, silently kicking myself for having brought in the photo and wishing I hadn't told her the truth. But the worst part was this wasn't a onetime situation.

This nonprofit also provided free books to kids through various events, such as books fairs, school functions, and health fairs. They had books for all ages covering a wide variety of topics and it was a fabulous way to encourage children to read. Most of the events took place in the evenings or on weekends, so they would always ask for volunteers. At first, I was happy to help. Being new to Los Angeles, I didn't know many people so I often didn't have plans that prevented me from attending these events.

Unfortunately, this colleague would sometimes work the same events. She would take these as another opportunity to bring up my family and preach to me. I would try, unsuccessfully, to change the subject. After a few events, I told her it made me uncomfortable and asked if we could just not talk about my family anymore. I'll never forget her telling me, "I'm not being offensive because homosexuality is a sin and I'm just telling you the truth." After that because I didn't always know what events she would attend, I stopped volunteering altogether.

I still had to see this coworker at the office and, for the next year, she would take any opportunity when we were alone together to raise the topic and give me another lecture. I could be standing in the break room heating my lunch or refilling my water bottle, it didn't matter. It got so bad that I would avoid her whenever possible.

I would cautiously walk up to the break room and pause before entering to hear who was there or delay my lunch if I couldn't grab my food from the fridge without encountering her.

After my first year, we moved offices, and Amanda and I shared one with a door. I was grateful for a physical barrier between me and the rest of the world. My second year, the site started to have financial issues. They were laying off staff and still struggling to pay those they retained. It felt a little selfish, but I wasn't upset when this colleague was eventually laid off.

It never ceases to amaze me the little things I've found to be a struggle over the years. The things most families never even think about can cause great apprehension, and they are things everyone should be able to say and do. Shouldn't I be able to decorate my workspace with a family photo without facing torment?

I debated taking down the family photo, but at that point the damage was done. The cat was out of the bag, and that year a woman who saw my photo as permission to exercise her personal mission made me miserable.

One of the most unfortunate things is that this was one of my favorite pictures of my family, and now every time I think about or look at it, I'm reminded of that year. I also learned a brutal lesson that day: don't share at work. That's where a person goes to do a job, and the people there don't have to be friends. They don't have to respect a coworker and, if they have a position of power, they may use it to make someone and their family feel like less, even if they have no right to do so. That was seven years ago, and I've never taken another family photo to work to decorate my desk.

I had about a month break between my first two years of service. In August 2010, I flew home to spend that time with my family.

Two nights before I was supposed to fly back to LA, Katie and I were at my mom's house for a family dinner. We were sitting in the den chatting and checking email as we waited for our dads to arrive. Our mom was flitting around as she barbecued chicken breasts.

Suddenly, there was a loud bang and she screamed from the kitchen, "The house is on fire! Oh my god! The house is on fire! Get out!"

Katie and I jumped into action. Katie called 911 while I grabbed the leash and got Boo, my mom's dog, out of the house. Once we were all outside, there was nothing we could do but watch as her home burned.

"Mom," I said gently, "I'm going to call Dad. I'm sure he and Jerry are already on the way and if they get to our street and see the commotion and the fire they're going to freak."

She was in such shock she didn't reply right away, "Huh, oh, yeah, right. We should do that."

I dialed his number, and he answered on the first ring. "We're on our way. We'll be there in a few minutes. Something's going on, we've been passed by two fire trucks already."

"Dad," I said, fighting to sound calm and together despite sobbing, "we all got out and are okay, but the house is on fire."

I heard a sharp intake of breath, "We'll be there in a minute. And you said everyone is out? Everyone's fine? No one's hurt?"

"Yeah, everyone's out. We're okay. Just in shock."

My dad arrived a few minutes later. He couldn't drive down the street with all the fire trucks and had to park at the end of the road. He and Jerry came running up to the house.

"Oh my god! What happened?" he asked as he and Jerry gave us hugs. We then stood there and cried together.

"I don't know," my mom stammered. "I was just cooking dinner. I was barbecuing and then there was this bang. I looked out the kitchen window and all I could see were huge flames." She broke down bawling, and my dad just held her for a minute.

Then he asked, "What can I do?" My dad called the insurance company and got somebody to meet us out there. The firefighters were amazing and asked what our most prized possessions were and tried to get them out of the house. It was a windy day, and by the time they got the fire under control, the entire house was ruined. They couldn't salvage much, but we appreciated the effort. They also gave us a donation from their Burnout Fund: a bag with toiletries and some cash to get us through the night. The insurance agent got us a room at a hotel that accepted animals.

Katie and I started to have issues with our asthma, so Jerry walked us down to the end of the street to the ambulance to be treated for smoke inhalation, which upset my mom even more, despite all our assurances that we would be fine.

Katie and I ended up being taken to the hospital to monitor our breathing. Jerry went with us and my dad brought my mom later after she'd finished dealing with the insurance agent for the night. After we got situated Jerry disappeared for a few minutes. "Where are you going?" I asked.

"I'm going to find you some booties. You can't just walk around all night without anything on your feet." In my haste, I'd run out of the house barefoot (when your house is on fire, shoes are the last thing on your mind). He returned with blue hospital booties and gently slipped them on my feet.

Despite the horrible events of the evening, it was wonderful to have family to depend on. Once my mom and dad made it to the hospital there were more tears. My mom really struggled with the fact that Katie and I were in the ER, even though we knew our asthma attacks weren't serious.

When we were finally discharged, I went to the hotel with my mom and dad to try to get Boo settled, look at the paperwork from the insurance agent, and make a plan for the next day. Katie and Jerry went to Walmart, the only store open late in our small city.

We had a few toiletries but no clothes except what we were wearing, and I still needed a real pair of shoes. We met back up at the hotel around midnight. Jerry and Katie had picked up some snacks, but no one was hungry.

Two days later, with our life still in shambles and knowing they would have to demolish and rebuild my mom's home, I got on a plane and flew back to Los Angeles. I had orientation starting for my second term, which I couldn't miss.

Much of my second year was spent missing my family and feeling bad I wasn't there for them in the way that I wanted to be. Getting on a plane less than forty-eight hours after the fire was one of the hardest things I've ever done. I wanted to be present for my mom as she dealt with losing almost everything, filing insurance paperwork, and rebuilding her home.

My mom and I spoke often after I returned to Los Angeles. She was feeling her mortality and aware of how lucky she was. It was determined the safety valve malfunctioned and her barbeque had exploded. It was one time we all appreciated her forgetfulness. She'd been out on the patio cooking and had just come into the house to grab something she'd left in the kitchen. If she'd been outside, the blast would've killed her. We were all aware of how close we came to losing her.

Aside from the negativity in the office, I enjoyed teaching ESL to the adults in the community. In the second year, I considered going back to school and getting an MA-TESOL, which is a master's degree in teaching English to speakers of other languages. I found a program I loved, but it would take one year to complete, not to mention it would be intense and cost about $45,000. I had no idea how I would pay for it but this became a moot point. Financial issues had caught up with the nonprofit. They eventually laid off the entire workforce aside from Amanda and me because they'd paid for our service upfront. Toward the end of my second year, they cut our adult ESL program. The possibility of having a full-time paid position at the end of my service no longer existed.

Sin

You stand there
With your religion
Your God
And stare
Back at me
And tell me
That I've sinned
You declare
That I can
Be saved
If I follow you
And your God
Your religion
But what can you
Save me from?
You speak of horrors
Of sex, drugs,
Hell on earth
Vulgar language
Scares you
I call you
A bitch, a whore
And you scream
Tell me that
I'm the Devil
And you run

Back to your shelter
Your religion
Your God
And I smile
I turn
And continue
My sinful life
And I laugh
Because you're right
I am the Devil

Part 3
Returning Home 2011-2015

9 Things Change

By the time my second AmeriCorps term ended in 2011, I'd been volunteering for three years. I was tired. Tired of working and volunteering for programs that didn't go smoothly, even when I had done good work. Tired of being poor, tired of struggling, and tired of the lack of stability. After two years in Los Angeles, I was determined I didn't want to work in a position where I had little power or an organization in which I had little respect for my coworkers. And I had decided I would never again stay in a work environment hostile toward my family.

I desperately needed change, but I was also terrified. For the first time, I didn't know what to do with myself. I had found a career I truly loved and yet, economically, it was a horrible time to find work in that field. While in Los Angeles, I watched several nonprofits go under and programs cut as thousands of teachers were laid off. I knew I still wanted to teach but couldn't justify spending $45,000 for a degree I might never be able to use. After three years of volunteering, broke and utterly defeated with the choices in front of me, I decided I needed to take some time to figure out my life. California was too expensive and, while I loved the weather, I hated the traffic.

It had been nine years since I'd fled my hometown to go to college on the East Coast. While I was grateful for all the amazing experiences and especially for the opportunities to travel, I missed my family. After being away during such a trying time, I really wanted to be closer to them and spend time with everyone. Since my path in life had been derailed, I knew it would take a while to figure out my next steps, so I returned to Idaho. For the first time in my adult life, I put down roots.

I moved back without any expectations for change. I thought I would return to the same close-mindedness I knew growing up. And while I wasn't excited about that prospect, my time in Los Angeles had taught me that even in some larger, more progressive locations, I could still experience discrimination. And while some areas are generally more accepting than others, no place is perfect. I realized some things may be outside of my control, but I do have the power to choose who I surround myself with.

After the difficulties with my previous position and being dirt poor after three years of volunteering, I was eager to find a "real" job that actually paid money. Given I was at a crossroads and didn't know what to do, I had low standards: find a job I didn't hate. I didn't have to love it, I didn't even have to like it, I just didn't want to hate my life for forty hours every week. I also needed health insurance.

I quickly applied for every job I found for which I was qualified. Several of the positions were at the same hospital where Jerry worked. It's one of the largest employers in the state, with many locations and clinics across Southern Idaho. It was never a given that the people reviewing my application or with whom I interviewed would know his name.

After a couple of interviews that didn't result in a job offer, I got a call for a position at the community cancer clinic. I was a bit nervous about the job; I almost didn't apply because the description specifically stated the employee would need to be comfortable working with patients who were dying. I wasn't sure I would have the strength for this situation. My only experience in health care was when I had worked at the OB/GYN office. Occasionally a patient would miscarry. A patient once spent the entire afternoon in the exam room bawling. Her grief was so great she didn't even have the strength to go home. Our physician, nurse, and other staff spent a lot of time with her, consoling her and discussing next steps. When she finally left, tears welled up in my eyes, and I watched her husband half carry her out of the office.

Despite my reservations, I went to the interview because I figured I had nothing to lose. There was no guarantee they would like me and even if they did, I didn't have to accept a job offer. Besides, it was common practice that if an interviewee wasn't the right fit for one position but had good skills overall, for the interviewer to mention this to HR. It was possible they could flag me as a potential candidate for other positions.

The interview had gone well. I walked of out the office and called my mom, "I hope they like me as much as I liked them, because I really want this job." The next few days were nerve-racking as I continued to apply for other jobs even though I was hoping this one would pan out. A few days later the clinic manager called and told me they really liked me and wanted to offer me the position. She explained it could take a couple of weeks before I heard from human resources because they had to check references and process the offer, but she wanted to let me know I was their top choice.

Because I wasn't working and didn't have to give notice, I could start immediately. When I began my orientation a few weeks later I was surprised that a couple of Jerry's friends, including one who had attended my dads' commitment ceremony in 1997, worked in the same clinic.

Jerry had worked in oncology when he was a floor nurse. Since the field is very specialized and requires additional training, most nurses stay in the field for the rest of their careers. He had a tight-knit group of friends when he worked on the inpatient floor. A couple of them had grown tired of the alternating shift work as they got older and wanted to move into the clinic setting where they could work regular days and hours. Two of Jerry's close friends had gone this route and now worked in the outpatient clinic.

The first couple of weeks it was funny when I ran into them. Neither one knew I was back in Boise, and they were surprised I was working at the clinic. Because we were old family friends, people noticed we knew each other and would ask how I'd met them.

When I mentioned they had worked with my dad back when they were all floor nurses, they would always ask his name. When I told them Jerry's name, they knew who he was. He had worked at the hospital for over twenty years by that time. When Jerry got into management he ran the scheduling department, which helped make hospital appointments for all the clinics, so most people at least knew him by name, even if they hadn't met him.

He left scheduling and worked for the community cancer clinic for a brief time before the director of the scheduling department offered him a large raise to come back, so some of the long-term staff had worked with him during his brief stint there.

During my second week, I got stopped in the hall by Angela, a loveable, assertive woman who'd worked there for years. "Natalie, I have a bone to pick with you!"

"Um, okay … what's up?"

"You just started working here, yet you seem to know everyone. What's going on?"

"Oh, well, it's not really that I know everyone. Some staff used to work with my dad Jerry on the floor years ago."

"Jerry? I know Jerry. He's amazing; I just love him! What's he up to now?"

Since Jerry had been out since high school, everyone at the hospital knew he was gay. Because we're not blood related, we don't share a last name or look anything alike, so people didn't know we're family until I started talking about his work at the hospital. I experienced a much easier time integrating into the clinic office than previous workplaces. Word spread through the gossip mill that I was Jerry's daughter. That took the stress away, and I didn't have to think about who I could mention my dads to because most people already knew I had a gay family.

I was surprised at the kindness and acceptance I received. Part of this may have been the culture of the hospital in general, but I also think oncology tends to be a more inclusive field. Cancer is a disease that doesn't discriminate, so the hospital and its employees can't afford to either. We saw patients from all backgrounds including LGBTQ, immigrants, refugees, and prisoners.

During my time there, I heard stories from other areas of the country where gay couples were denied their rights at health care institutions. I remember hearing about a couple in another state who was told a nurse didn't want to care for them because they were gay. This sparked a lot of conversation at our institution and specifically at our clinic. Nurses were outraged that someone in their field would treat a patient in that manner.

One of them, Melissa, opened up to me one day about her feelings. "I just don't get it, Natalie. We have an obligation to care for our patients. We can't choose who to treat."

"I know, you're preaching to the choir," I said.

"I have to tell you about a situation I encountered in a previous position where I was caring for a prisoner. He needed ongoing care and was brought to the hospital on a regular basis because the treatment wasn't offered in the prison medical ward."

"Okay," I said, not sure where the story was going.

"When I worked with prisoners, I never wanted to know what

they'd done to land them in jail. It was just easier to treat them if I didn't know. But one day the prison guard mentioned the patient was imprisoned because he had raped and murdered two teenage girls."

"Oh, wow," I said. "That had to be hard to hear. What did you do?"

"It was hard, Natalie. It was horrible. As the mother of two girls myself, that news tormented me. For a moment, I didn't want to treat the patient anymore. But at the same time, it was my job to care for this person. No matter what he'd done or what type of person he was, he still deserved the same medical care as everyone else," she said. "So with that reminder to myself, I continued to do my work."

I am in no way comparing homosexuality to rape and murder. I mention this because it's an extreme example. I think everyone would agree rape and murder are morally and ethically wrong. Most people would even say they find the actions of the prisoner offensive. However, even in this situation, where there is no debate, this nurse recognized her responsibility to treat everyone with dignity and respect.

What I don't understand is how some people say they can recognize the necessity to provide people with equal treatment under the law but then say it only applies in certain situations. People still use their religion and morality as an excuse to deny services to those perceived as *other*. In some cases it's medical care, in others it's denying a job, housing, service at a restaurant, or even recognition of their family.

But when we live in a country where we say *everyone* is treated equally, we don't get to cherry-pick who that applies to. We can't say it's justifiable to deny some people their rights because we personally find something offensive. People have the right to their beliefs and they have the right to think that homosexuality is wrong, but they don't have the right to use their religion and their beliefs to deny the rights of others.

While overall people in the clinic were accepting of my family, I quickly learned to be careful around some. I walked into the break room one day to a coworker talking about how homosexuality was a sin and how he didn't understand why people would want to legalize gay marriage. He was also one of the few people who didn't know about my gay family.

He was finishing his lunch, so I had a seat at another table with a colleague who looked at me as she uncomfortably shifted in her seat. Trish tried to end the conversation and get Paul to change the subject, but he just raised his voice.

"Homosexuality is unnatural and it damages our children. By allowing gays to marry, we're telling our children this behavior that goes again God is acceptable and it's not."

As this point, Trish didn't say anything; I think she was afraid that if she kept talking so would he.

A few minutes later Paul finished eating and left the room, leaving just Trish and me.

"I'm sorry, Natalie," she said as soon as the door closed.

"It's okay. I mean, it's not *okay*. It's actually a great example of why people shouldn't discuss things like religion and politics at work, especially in an open space like the break room. He has no idea how other people feel about the issue and there's a high chance others may not agree when you talk about these things in a space like this. It's really disrespectful of him, but that's who he is and I'm not going to get in an argument with someone at work. It's just a great example of some of the situations families like mine deal with because society says we're different."

"And you shouldn't have to," she responded.

"I appreciate you acknowledging that. We're making progress, but we still have a long way to go."

I found my hesitance about working with dying patients unnecessary. After starting work, I realized how growing up in a closeted gay family enabled me to compartmentalize well. Being in situations where we had to learn to read people and adjust our behavior based on how others would react taught me to be adaptable. Working in a cancer clinic was an emotional roller coaster. I'd have a patient who was elated to find out their cancer was gone and five minutes later a patient who was just given an estimate of only a few weeks to live. It turned out that being flexible and able to easily acclimate to new situations based on the environment and feelings of the family was a skill that equipped me for my job.

※

In addition to working a job I truly enjoyed, I was happy to be home with family. By the time I returned, my mom's house had been rebuilt, and she'd moved in to her new home. The only positive thing to come from the fire was that she finally got the granite countertops she'd always wanted.

During my parents' divorce and the years after, our philosophy has always been to lean on each other during the tough times and to work through them as a family. Because of the strong relationship Katie and I have with our parents, we enjoy spending time with them, even as adults.

For years, my family had a standing coffee date at the local Starbucks on Saturday mornings. People would show up if able and hang out for as long as they could. Sometimes it would be thirty minutes, other times we'd sit there for a couple of hours. I fell into their normal routine of weekly coffee dates and occasional family dinners. One of my favorite things about returning to Idaho was being able to see my family in person and participating in the activities that I'd missed out on for so long.

I also got to spend more one-on-one time with my dad. He loved to set up lunch dates with my sister and me during the week. It would sometimes take a bit of coordinating to find time when I could take a longer lunch and step out of the clinic, but it was always a nice treat. When I was younger, Jerry used to work later than my dad. I used to get home from school, and my dad and I would watch the news together and discuss politics as he cooked dinner. I had missed these conversations while living outside Idaho.

I was also happy to spend Christmas with my family again. While I'd come home from the holiday when I lived in Los Angeles, I'd missed a few holidays while living overseas. My dad has always exchanged gifts with his judicial assistant. My first year back home, she gave us a movie basket that included a five-pound bag of peanut M&M's. Katie and I had gone over to my dads' place a couple of days later to hang out and watch *Modern Family* together. This show had become a staple, as it was the first time we'd seen a family like ours on mainstream TV.

"Jerry, where're the M&M's?" I asked as I looked through the pantry.

"Um, well, your dad and I …" he started.

"Oh, no you don't!" my dad interrupted. "You don't get to blame any of this on me," he said laughing.

"Any of what? What did you do, Jerry?" Katie asked.

"Well, they're gone," he said.

"Gone! It was a five-pound bag!"

"I know, Natalie, I couldn't help it. I just started eating them. And the next thing I knew, they were gone."

"Okay, well, Katie and I are coming over this weekend for a movie night. Are you going to buy more?"

"Yes, I'm going to grab another big bag before then."

When we showed up Friday night for dinner and the movie, Jerry announced, "Let's run to the store to get some M&M's."

"I thought you'd bought some already," Katie mentioned. My dad started laughing in the kitchen.

Jerry turned red. "Well, I might have bought some after you were here the other night."

"And …" Katie pressed.

"And I might have eaten them," Jerry confessed.

Katie and I just stared at him for a minute. "So let me get this straight," I started. "You ate ten pounds of peanut M&M's in a week?"

"Natalie, be nice! You know how I am. I can't have them around because I just keep eating them."

"Is that why we have to go to the store? To buy a third bag?" Katie asked. "You were waiting until the night of so you couldn't eat them before the movie."

His face turned a shade darker. "That might have had something to do with it," he answered sheepishly.

Being back home also gave me the opportunity to build closer relationships with some of my other relatives. Grandma Sharon lived close by and so did many of my cousins on Jerry's side of the family. I'd missed several family get-togethers and reunions, and being back in the same city meant I could bond with extended family in the Boise area.

Since I hadn't lived in Idaho for a long time and I'd only kept in touch with a couple of people from high school, I didn't have many friends when I returned. In an effort to meet new people, I perused the website Meetup and joined a few groups.

One of the first events I went to was a monthly book club. It was a small group with six to eight people attending. I was originally looking for groups with people my own age. I've always been told I'm mature for my age, and I've often had friends who are older than me, so age generally isn't a factor when I'm looking to meet new friends. However, since I was concerned about how accepting people would be in Boise, I figured I had a better shot of finding people who wouldn't object to my family if I sought out people in the younger generation.

This club had a wide variety of ages from millennials to retirees. One of the things I loved about being in a book club was the discussion. We discussed the plot and the characters in the books, but we also learned a lot about each other because we talked about how our experiences affected our perception of the book. It took me a few months to get comfortable with everyone. But once we started reading books that had gay characters or dealt with issues of discrimination, I ventured into sharing about my family.

Since we read books that asked challenging questions, we also sometimes had difficult conversations. There was a high level of respect in the group. Everyone's opinion was allowed; we didn't always agree, but that generally led to more questions. And while people talked openly and asked for clarifications on others' views, it never transformed into a debate.

After attending the group for a couple of years, our organizer moved out of state, and they asked if I would take over. I was excited to do so. I was familiar with the group and its members, but I also wanted to try to expand attendance.

Through the same site, I also joined a Spanish conversation group. Now that I was no longer teaching, I wasn't using my Spanish daily and didn't want to lose my skills. Before I could attend any events, the group organizer stepped down. Since I had an interest in the group, I took over as organizer and immediately started scheduling monthly events.

Both groups started to grow. I met some people I really clicked with and started hanging out with them outside events. The more people I met and started to be honest with, the easier it became. I got used to saying "my dads" in public or when talking to new people. I would often be able to tell how comfortable people were by their reactions. The more I used this technique, the more pleasantly surprised I was to see many didn't respond with silence or involuntary facial expressions of disdain. Most people I met didn't care much at all anymore.

My new friends were all accepting of my family, although most weren't Idaho natives. A lot of people move to Idaho from other states because the cost of living is low and there's a relaxed culture with easy access to a variety of outdoor activities. Many natives complain about the influx of people, particularly those from California. But I've become grateful for these transplants because they're helping to change the climate when it comes to the LGBTQ community.

Lost

All these years of pain and hate
Are slowly starting to deteriorate
I try to write with pen in hand
But from my mind I can't demand
Words of feeling and emotion
Words that cause a contradiction
I hide from this side of me
Saying it's not what I'm to be
But words of joy still don't flow
My mind has nowhere to go
I tried so hard to free my soul
That I have lost my main goal
To always be true to no one but me
For once I'm blinded—I cannot see
I've lost my light that showed the way
Lost my courage and decided to stay
Here in this world that I perceive
To be full of fake people who deceive
I've lost my faith and God too
I keep trying to restore and renew
But I've also lost hope that I'll ever return
To that person whose soul once burned
Burned with a passion not understood
But looked upon as a person who would
Get lost in herself and not know why
Turn into the others and slowly die

Die without knowing her own pain
Or the life she lived in vain
But I'm still living and finally awake
And I know my life was not a mistake
I realize now that I can fight
And only I can restore the light
I haven't completely lost my soul
Just slightly decided to change my goal
As for faith, I've nothing yet to renew
I'm simply evaluating my pledge to You
And, yes, I think I still have hope
I'm just making excuses, trying to cope
For the first time with the fact
That my emotion I'm beginning to lack
I've lost the connection with my heart
For a while there, I was torn apart
But losses can be regained
When one becomes in touch with the pain
Pain and joy of the world combined
A pain and joy that are only mine
Hopefully now I'll become in touch
With a heart and soul I miss much
And see, I haven't lost my hope
Just lost the knowledge of how to cope

10 Gay Marriage

My dad was appointed to the court just after his twenty-seventh birthday as one of the youngest judges ever chosen. A year later, the legislature passed minimum standards requiring five years of practice as a lawyer to be a magistrate judge. The legislature enacted a grandfather clause to keep my dad on the bench. Since he was in an elected position, they couldn't just throw him off even though he didn't meet the new requirements. After that, he spent months with his friends and lawyers calling him grandpa despite only being twenty-eight years old at the time. In 1993, he was appointed to the Idaho State Court of Appeals by then governor, Cecil D. Andrus. My dad served four terms as chief judge.

As a state judge, he faced reelection every six years. His first election was in 1994 before he came out to our family. However, he was up again in 2000 and 2006. Fortunately, he was always unopposed, but the time leading up to each election was stressful. He was concerned someone would run against him and then he would be outed in the midst of the campaign. He always breathed a sigh of relief when the deadline passed and no one had challenged him. He would have been up for re-election again in 2012, but he had already partially retired.

I had always thought my dad would work forever. He loved his job, and Jerry is ten years younger than him. Since they couldn't legally marry, they had no access to each other's retirement benefits, which meant they were both responsible for their own retirement and financial planning.

But in 2009, my dad turned fifty-five and found himself in a unique position. Due to spending twenty-eight years on the bench, he qualified for early retirement. He decided to take advantage of the opportunity and went on senior status, which meant he only had to work a total of thirty-five days each year for five years. He could then fully retire in 2014. After going on senior status, he received the Kramer Award, the top award in the judicial branch and given by the Supreme Court.

My dad's early retirement caught everyone in the family off guard. Because no one expected him to retire for years, we were a little concerned about how he would handle the transition. My dad is extremely type A and relaxing isn't exactly his forte. He continued to get up at five every morning and head to the office for a few hours. Then he'd go to the gym. Eventually, he started volunteering at a local nonprofit. He was also able to pick up a few extra hours at the court by working on various projects. Splitting his time into a few hours every day seemed to help him phase out work.

The biggest difference was that with his retirement, he no longer had to run for reelection. For the first time since he'd come out to our family, no one was worried about him losing his job. My dad seemed to adjust to his new situation much faster than the rest of us. Once he no longer worried about keeping his job, he would introduce Jerry to new acquaintances as his partner. At first, this would surprise Jerry. He'd grown so accustomed to his perfected disappearing act that he'd already started to turn away before hearing my dad's introduction and realizing it was okay for him to stay. With this change, Jerry finally got the chance to publicly share his relationship.

It wasn't until after my dad went on senior status in 2009 that he took Jerry on another work trip in our state. They had become close with another judge and his wife and decided to invite them over to the house—the first time they'd done so with someone in the legal field from Idaho. They became friends and both couples attended a conference in Coeur d'Alene.

My dad would later contrast his experiences in Idaho with those he and Jerry had elsewhere. As a chief judge, he had attended national conferences in several cities including Seattle, New Orleans, Washington D.C., Santa Fe, and San Francisco. At these conferences, he met chief judges from other states, and he also met Justices Scalia, Kennedy, Roberts, Alito, and Ginsburg of the United States Supreme Court.

One of Jerry and Dad's favorite trips was to Washington, D.C. where they got to see the private reception hall in the Supreme Court building, which housed marble busts of every chief justice who had ever served on court. It was also during one of these trips when Jerry started joking he was a judge's wife. While the judges attended their sessions, the spouses would often go on tours together. Jerry was usually the only man in a large group of wives.

My dads saw diversity on the court when they met judges of different racial and ethnic backgrounds, and at times my dad was even told by other judges how happy they were to see them display another element of diversity represented in the court system by a high-level gay judge. During these trips my dads were always welcomed, respected, and treated fairly.

Katie and I could also finally be more open. For years, we hadn't been able to share anything about our family on Facebook. We couldn't post family photos from the holidays. With privacy settings we could restrict it to our friends, but we never knew who they'd talk to or share with so we were always guarded. For months after my dad had started to be more open, Katie and I would continue to ask permission when we wanted to mention something family related in our status update.

Even though we were now all in the same city, my dad kept up with his daily family emails, and on May 13, 2014, he announced he and Jerry were planning to go to the courthouse that Friday to be one of the first couples to legally marry in Idaho. Hours earlier the court had announced its verdict and struck down the ban on gay marriage in the state. He and Jerry carried on a hurried discussion and decided to be a part of history.

We were all shocked and elated at the news. For years, I had been convinced *I* would see the legalization of gay marriage, but I was unsure whether my dads would live to witness it. Generally, change is slow. None of us expected the snowball that had occurred over the past few years.

President Barack Obama did more than any other president to advance the cause of equal rights for the LGBTQ community. In December 2010, the repeal of the "Don't Ask, Don't Tell" policy allowed gay men and women to serve openly in the military. A few months later in February 2011, his administration announced they would no longer defend the Defense of Marriage Act (DOMA), which defined marriage as a union between a man and woman. He was also the first president to acknowledge LGBTQ Pride Month as well as take action to extend federal hate crime laws to cover the LGBTQ community and promote protections for people who are transgender. He also signed an executive order barring discrimination in the workplace against federal employees.[1]

There were battles in several courts across the country to legalize same-sex marriage. The LGBTQ community was inspired not only by changes in some state laws but also the change in the attitude of the federal government under the Obama Administration.

We only had a few days' notice, so I immediately contacted my boss. I apologized for the short notice, explained the situation, and asked if there was any way I could take Friday morning off.

She didn't even hesitate. "Congratulations, Natalie! Of course you have to be there. Don't worry about it; we'll figure out the coverage. You can't miss your dads' wedding. Tell your dads congratulations too. I'm so happy for all of you."

My mom and sister had similar support in their offices as well and got the morning off without any issues. My dads started planning their wedding while my mom, Katie, and I started discussing how we could make their wedding special with three days' notice.

But less than twenty-four hours before we headed to the courthouse, a stay was issued. No marriages licenses would be issued in Idaho while our governor fought the decision. When I went into work Friday morning instead of going to the courthouse, a friend, colleague, and LGBTQ ally stopped me in the hallway. With tears streaming down her face she gave me a huge hug.

"I'm so sorry Natalie. I just can't believe this. I really thought it was going to happen today."

I couldn't help but cry as well. Her support and encouragement were so powerful, especially because I was completely devastated that once again my family was being treated as though we had second-class status.

"I thought it would happen today too. I know we'll get there. It's just hard to be so close and have it ripped away. Honestly, I never thought this would happen in my dads' lifetime, so we're getting there faster than any of us expected, but it still seems so slow in some ways."

Adding to the difficulties was the governor's pledge to continue to fight marriage equality. On the thirteenth of May, in response to the strike down of the ban, Governor Otter issued the following statement: "In 2006, the people of Idaho exercised their fundamental right, reaffirming that marriage is the union of a man and a woman. Today's decision, while disappointing, is a small setback in a long-term battle that will end at the U.S. Supreme Court. I am firmly committed to upholding the will of the people and defending our Constitution."[2]

In the week that followed, he issued three more statements reiterating his stance that marriage should be a union between one man and one woman and showed his support for the stay. He pledged to continue to challenge the original decision that had struck down the ban of same-sex marriage. One of his press releases stated they would go before the judge "with arguments that go to the heart of Idaho's values and respect for the family unit as it's been embraced by society for millennia."[3]

The words of an elected official who was supposed to represent all of Idaho's residents acted as a dagger. It hurt that he would so easily brush aside LGBTQ families. Once again, our family unit was invalidated by this government official who was supposed to represent, support, and protect all of his constituents.

Two months later, my dad officially retired. He and Jerry had been watching to see how things would play out in the courts, but there was no time estimate. Several states were fighting similar cases and everyone knew that it would eventually end up at the Supreme Court, but we had no idea how long that would take and if the highest court would agree to hear the case.

My dads decided to move forward with planning their wedding. The dominoes had started to fall. We all knew it would only be a matter of time before gay marriage was legal in our state. With the unknown timeline in Idaho, my dads decided to roll out a wedding announcement. They would legally marry on January 18, 2015, which would be on the eighteenth anniversary of their original commitment ceremony: *18 on the 18th.*

They also started to consider joining the lawsuit if the Supreme Court hadn't decided on the issue by the time they were wed.

They originally discussed returning to San Francisco and getting legally married in the same church they'd had their commitment ceremony. While both of their dads had passed years earlier, both of their moms were still alive, and they wanted to make sure they could attend. By this time, Grandma Izzy was in her eighties and travel was challenging. So my dads decided to have the ceremony in Vancouver, Washington where gay marriage was legal. Plus, the location would be easily accessible for everyone.

Like most weddings, theirs involved months of planning. They needed to find the right venue (one that accepted gay couples), choose colors, pick a menu, rent tuxes, as well as decide on bridesmaid dresses for Katie and me. I'm still not a huge fan of dresses so shopping was painful, but Katie and Jerry both mentioned afterward how well I tolerated it, especially when, after a full day of shopping, we ended up getting dresses from the first place we had looked. Shopping with a gay dad can be hard work, but at least he was adamant we find something Katie and I both loved, felt comfortable in, and could wear again.

The most entertaining part of the wedding planning was when Jerry mentioned ring shopping.

"We have rings, Jerry," my dad said.

"Yes, but we need upgrades," Jerry responded with pleading eyes. It's a joke in our family that whatever Jerry wants, Jerry gets, so of course, in the end, they bought upgrades.

They were in the middle of all the planning when, on the seventh of October, the Ninth Circuit issued the decision to strike down the same-sex marriage ban in Idaho. Joy once again spread across Boise and the LGBTQ community. Couples planned to go to the courthouse to get married the next day as the decision stated marriage licenses would be issued immediately. But there was confusion as Governor Otter issued a statement that despite their decision, the stay was still in place. "Today's decision by the 9th Circuit is disappointing, but not unexpected. I will carefully evaluate the opinion, along with yesterday's surprising decision by the U.S. Supreme Court, and talk with legislative leaders and the Attorney General before determining our path forward. The stay on same-sex marriage in Idaho remains in effect until we are directed otherwise by the 9th Circuit."[4]

The next morning, Justice Kennedy issued another stay preventing marriages from beginning immediately. Governor Otter responded to this decision as well, expressing his pleasure and vowing to continue work to try to protect "traditional marriage."[5] Two days later the stay was lifted, and Governor Otter again expressed his displeasure but agreed to comply with the law.

Couples flocked to the courthouse on Friday the tenth of October. Pastors from LGBTQ-friendly churches went to officiate the weddings free of charge. A large crowd gathered outside with people handing out flowers to couples as they left the courthouse and blowing bubbles in celebration. It was a beautiful day. While I couldn't go because of my work schedule, my dad stood outside and hugged each and every one of his friends as they walked by as newly married couples.

Unfortunately, Otter was still unwilling to stand down. On the twenty-first of October, he asked for an en banc review. He stated the three judges who had ruled on the case made "critical errors" and requested that the full panel of eleven judges from the Ninth Circuit reconsider their decision. The court declined his request.[6]

The battle for marriage equality sparked quite a few conversations in our family, especially when we met for weekly coffee dates. We often discussed our strength and resiliency, and it was during this time that Katie and I shared with our parents how grateful we were that our dad had come out to us. Despite all the ups and downs, we'd rather have known about his sexuality and grown up in the closet than have had our parents lie to us all of these years about the reason for their divorce.

Three months later, our family was on its way to Vancouver for my dads' wedding. We spent a couple of days taking care of last-minute details and attending the rehearsal dinner. Finally, it was the big day. Everyone got ready at the hotel and then we climbed into a couple of taxis to head to the venue. Given there would be an open bar, we had decided no one should be driving home at the end of the night.

My dad and Jerry spent a few minutes adding final touches to the decorations. They'd brought some tokens from their home. They had many to choose from. Their house can be sickening sweet with its *Always Kiss Me Goodnight* sign above the bed or LOML letters lying around that stand for *Love of My Life*. They finally settled on a photo collage from their original ceremony and two plaques: *Still in Love after All This Time* and *This is Our Happily Ever After*. And my aunt had crafted one of a kind *Mr. & Mr.* signs to decorate the entryway and tables for the reception.

Since both of their dads had passed on, Jerry made little boxes that held a photo of each. They were small enough to tuck in their pockets so they could carry their dads with them during the ceremony. This was a surprise to my dad and started him crying just before the wedding.

My dad wore a pin from his Grandma Tortosa for his *something old*. It had been passed down through the generations and had eventually been given to him. He'd wore it on his tux during their original ceremony in 1997. They also had to be a little silly, so they wore brightly colored socks. Jerry's had polka dots while my dad wore crazy stripes.

They wanted to have their moms walk them down the aisle, but my dad didn't want Grandma Izzy to have any anxiety over this. Fortunately, there were two rooms: one for the bride and one for the groom. Since we had two grooms, they gave the other room to their moms, Katie, and me. We just hung out before the ceremony. My dad came to get Grandma Izzy to walk her to her seat, which started the ceremony.

They played "A Thousand Years" by Christina Perri as they marched down the aisle, which was fitting considering how long it took for them to get to this point. Their vows were incredibly sweet: "Welcome! The date: January 18, 1997. The place: Trinity Episcopal Church, San Francisco, California. The Time: The Federal government passes the Defense of Marriage Act in 1996 and thirty-eight states, including Idaho, pass constitutional amendments banning gay marriage. For one new couple two things are clear: First, they would never be allowed to get legally married; Second, they would spend the rest of their lives together. Whereas they couldn't have been more wrong on the first, time has proven and strengthened the truth of the second."

Katie sang "Ave Maria" and I read from *The Prophet*. After the exchanging of the rings and the announcement of *Mr. & Mr.* the wedding ended with them walking out as "At Last" by Etta James played in the background.

The wedding was followed by an incredible reception. Katie and I got to sign the marriage certificate as witnesses. Appetizers were served along with a three-course meal. It was definitely the fanciest wedding I've ever been to, with monogrammed napkins and personalized mint tins for all the guests. After the meal, plenty of dancing took place. Grandma Izzy even went out on the dance floor with her walker. Later they cut the cake, which had two groomsmen on it. Of course, only one groomsman was on top. The other was climbing up the side, with his hand outstretched. My dads liked to joke this was Jerry trying to make his way to the top, and my dad was trying to decide whether to lend him a hand.

My dads' wedding was one of the happiest and proudest days

of my life. Our family had waited so long for this moment and had spent so many years being told we were undeserving of this basic right. But for me there was a sense of validation because after eighteen years, I was finally able to stand with my two dads when they legally wed.

There was also the realization that this was bigger than just our family. This wedding was a symbol to members of the younger generation, people like my gay cousin, a symbol that they will grow up in a world where marriage is a basic human right for all and a possibility for him and his friends. My hope is that the generation of kids growing up in gay families now will know a kinder and more accepting world.

People

People
Too large, too small
Too short, too tall
Too fat, too thin
Too many beliefs within
Too strong, too weak
Our dreams we seek
Too gay, too straight
How can we humiliate
Too sweet, too mean
With all these different perceptions
How can we be so unaccepting?

Reflections

After the wedding, my dads moved to Palm Springs. They'd been unable to relocate until after my dad retired because the bar is state specific. As a state judge, he was only able to practice in Idaho. When my dad was on the bench, he and Jerry lived by the saying, "Those who know, don't care. Those who care, don't know." They are now in an environment where they no longer must hide anything about themselves. They are both publicly out and active in their community. I believe both have a sense of freedom living in an area with a large LGBTQ community.

My mom, sister, and I are still in Idaho. While I've found the state has changed, we still have a long way to go. Katie and I may feel comfortable wearing our Queerspawn shirts and marching in the local Pride parade, but our governor continues to disagree with marriage equality and fight against transgender rights. We've also been unsuccessful in our campaign to add the words *sexual orientation* and *gender identity* to the existing Idaho Human Rights Act (IHRA) for over ten years now.[1] There is a lack of understanding in our local community about the importance of the Add the Words campaign, which started in 2006.[2] Many people believe the LGBTQ community is looking for *special* rights instead of *equal* rights.

I decided I wanted to write this book during the summer of 2015. I was taking a travel writing class online when I realized this was really the book that I wanted to be writing. I wrote a query letter for an assignment and then sent it to my family asking for their thoughts. While this is very much a book told from my perspective, it's also my family's story. For me, it was very important they were okay with me sharing our story with the world. We had several long conversations over the course of two months.

The most important conversation would be with my dad. He was the one who would be publicly outed by publishing our story. "Natalie, I only have one question: Why do you want to write this book?"

"I want to help people," I answered. "I want to help gay families by showing them what my closeted family has been through and some of the particular issues their children may face growing up with LGBTQ parents. And I want to help those straight people who still don't understand the LGBTQ community and their families. I want to educate people so we can reduce some of the hate by showing people those attitudes are the only things that actually harm kids with LGBTQ parents."

After listening to my reasons, my dad gave me his permission. "I'm comfortable with our story and I trust you to write and share it, although I would like to read it before you start sending it to publishers." And then he said something I will never forget, "They can't hurt us anymore."

After twenty years of living in a gay family, what's my message? I'd like to say that I don't have any anger anymore, but that's not true. While I've dealt with everything from the past, the present can still make me mad. The current political climate is a struggle for me. Every time someone in public office actively tries to limit our rights, it upsets me. And any time someone tries to speak *for* me as a person with gay dads, it frustrates me. Over the years, I've heard people say I should be depressed, suicidal, and an addict simply because I grew up in a home with two men.

The truth is, I have gay dads and I'm not damaged. I grew up with an incredible and loving family that always provided for me when I was younger and has continued to guide and support me as I've grown older. And for the record, I have a voice and am perfectly capable of speaking for myself. The problem is that no one is asking. Yet, almost every day I hear news of someone with a position of authority talking about the detriments of gay parenting. The next time our public officials want to talk about how having LGBTQ parents affects their children, I invite them to speak with me. I'd be happy to share how we can improve our government policies so they are more inclusive of all families.

But the reality is I have been challenged. Facing others who constantly tell me my family isn't the same as others, that I'm somehow less, does have an effect. But for those who truly care about "the kids" and want to make sure life isn't more difficult for them, there is one easy fix: take a long hard look in the mirror. What are you doing to hurt gay families? What hateful messages do you spread? What homophobic rhetoric do you use? What actions do you take with the intent of harming those different from you? Because the only injury kids with gay parents endure is caused by the close-mindedness their families face by society.

It's no longer acceptable to tell LGBTQ families they don't matter. In fact, it never was okay, but previously our country seemed to be in a place where many people didn't understand that. I'm not telling anyone they have to think homosexuality is *right*. But I expect those who think it's a sin to do so without being hateful. People have the right to their opinions. But I also have the right to my family. No one in our country should be put in the situation where they grow up in fear because our society has decided some people are valued less than others. Kids shouldn't grow up in a world where being bullied, living a life of lies, and hostile work environments are the norm.

I have learned a lot from my experiences and from sharing my story with others. I am a stronger, more patient, tolerant, and accepting person due to my upbringing. The challenges my family has endured have made me realize how lucky I am to have a family so loving and open. Those experiences have also given me a calling to be an advocate and add my voice in the fight for our rights.

※

Where can we go from here? The words of Holocaust survivor Elie Wiesel provide food for thought. "The opposite of love is not hate, it's indifference."[3] If you aren't part of the LGBTQ community, stand as an ally. Tell us that you support us and will protect us against discrimination.

Wiesel reminds us that "We must always take sides. Neutrality helps the oppressor, never the victim. Silence encourages the tormentor, never the tormented."[4] Ask yourself, "What am I doing to advocate for gay families?" When they move into your neighborhood, do you welcome them? Do you allow your kids to play with theirs? Do you teach your kids that they should respect those who are different, even if they don't totally understand their lifestyle?

Finally, Wiesel pointed out that "There may be times when we are powerless to prevent injustice, but there must never be a time when we fail to protest."[5] We have made progress over the last couple of decades, but there is still a long way to go. Your voice is just as important as those in the LGBTQ community. You can speak up where some might be too terrified of personal injury to do so.

Please, stand with us, support us, but most of all, love us and teach your children: Love is Love.

Notes

Chapter 2: Blending Families
1. 104th Congress of the United States of America, Public Law 104–199—SEPT. 21, 1996
2. Wolf, "Timeline"
3. Government Publishing Office [US], 10 U.S.C. § 654

Chapter 6: Europe
1. *Anne Frank House*, Galesloot, ed.
2. *Homomonument*, Pink Point
3. Let's Go Budget Amsterdam, 59
4. Marcuse, Legacies of Dachau, 353
5. Dachau Concentration Camp, Distel, et al., eds.

Chapter 7: Peace Corps
1. Peace Corps, LGBTQ Volunteers

Chapter 10: Gay Marriage
1. "Advancing Social Progress," The Record
2. State of Idaho, "Governor Otter Reacts"
3. State of Idaho, "Governor Otter Seeks"
4. State of Idaho, "Federal Appeals Court"
5. State of Idaho, "Justice Kennedy Stays"

6. State of Idaho, "Governor Otter Asks"

Reflections
1. Idaho Legislature. Title 67, Chapter 59
2. Gough, Pavesic. "Add the Words"
3. Bult, Laura, "Nobel Peace Prize"
4. Tognotti, Chris, "5 Elie Wiesel Quotes"
5. Wiesel, Elie, "Nobel Lecture"

Bibliography

"Advancing Social Progress and Equality." The Record, *The White House: President Barack Obama*, accessed March 9, 2017, https://obamawhitehouse.archives.gov/the-record/social-progress.

Anne Frank House: A Museum with a Story. Edited by Hansje Galesloot. Translated by Lorraine T. Miller. Amsterdam, Anne Frank House, 2001.

Buehler, Kinston, Burke. *Let's Go Budget Amsterdam*. Harvard Student Agencies Inc. Cambridge, MA. 2012. Print.

Bult, Laura. "Nobel Peace Prize Winner Elie Wiesel's Best Quotes on Survival, Activism and Humanity. *New York Daily News*, July 2, 2016. http://www.nydailynews.com/news/world/elie-wiesel-quotes-survival-spirituality-humanity-article-1.2697132.

The Dachau Concentration Camp 1933-1945. Edited by Barbara Distel, Gabriele Hammermann, Stanislav Zámečník, and Jürgen Zarusky, Zdenek Zofka. Dachau: Comité International de Dachau, 2005.

DADT. 10 U.S.C. § 654. Government Publishing Office [US]. Accessed March 27, 2017.

https://www.gpo.gov/fdsys/pkg/USCODE-2010-title10/pdf/USCODE-2010-title10-subtitleA-partII-chap37-sec654.pdf.

Defense of Marriage Act (DOMA). Public Law 104–199—SEPT. 21, 1996. 104th Congress of the United States of America. Accessed March 27, 2017.

https://www.congress.gov/104/plaws/publ199/PLAW-104publ199.pdf.

Gough, Pavesic. "Add the Words." MDG Films, Quicksand Productions. (2014). Film.

Homomonument: In the Centre of Amsterdam. Amsterdam, Pink Point, n.d.

Marcuse, Harold. *Legacies of Dachau: The Uses and Abuses of a Concentration Camp, 1933-2001.* Cambridge: Cambridge University Press, 2001.

Idaho Human Rights Act. 67-5909. State Government and State Affairs Commission on Human Rights. Accessed March 28, 2017.

https://legislature.idaho.gov/statutesrules/idstat/title67/t67ch59/sect67-5909/

Peace Corps. *LGBTQ Volunteers.* Accessed February 24, 2017. http://files.peacecorps.gov/multimedia/pdf/learn/howvol/faq/LGBTQ_FAQs.pdf.

State of Idaho. "Federal Appeals Court Rejects Idaho Prohibition on Same-Sex Marriage." News release, October 7, 2014. https://gov.idaho.gov/mediacenter/press/pr2014/10%20October/pr_58.html.

"Governor Otter Asks Federal Appeals Court for En Banc Review of Marriage Ruling." News release, October 21, 2014. https://gov.idaho.gov/mediacenter/press/pr2014/10%20October/pr_63.html.

"Governor Otter Reacts to Court Ruling on Idaho's Same-Sex Marriage Ban." News release, May 13, 2014. https://gov.idaho.gov/mediacenter/press/pr2014/5.%20May/pr_029.html.

"Governor Otter Seeks Emergency Stay on Same-Sex Ruling." News release, May 14, 2014. https://gov.idaho.gov/mediacenter/press/pr2014/5.%20May/pr_030.html.

"Justice Kennedy Stays Appellate Court Mandate on Same-Sex Marriage in Idaho." News release, October 8, 2014. https://gov.idaho.gov/mediacenter/press/pr2014/10%20October/pr_59.html

Tognotti, Chris. "5 Elie Wiesel Quotes About the Holocaust." *Bustle,* July 2, 2016. https://www.bustle.com/articles/170489-5-elie-wiesel-quotes-about-the-holocaust.

Wiesel, Elie. "Nobel Lecture." NobelPrize.org. December 11, 1986. http://www.nobelprize.org/nobel_prizes/peace/laureates/1986/wiesel-lecture.html.

Wolf, Richard. "Timeline: Same-Sex Marriage Through the Years." *USA Today,* June 26, 2015, http://www.usatoday.com/story/news/politics/2015/06/24/same-sex-marriage-timeline/29173703/.